Bengal Cats: Your Guide for First Time Owners

Bengal Cats Unleashed: Care, Personality, Training, and Wild Daily Adventures

Helen Renisch

Disclaimer

The information contained in this book is based on the author's personal experiences as a Bengal cat owner. It is intended for educational and entertainment purposes only. The advice, tips, and recommendations shared are not a substitute for professional veterinary care, animal behavior consultation, or other professional services.

Every Bengal cat is unique, and what works for one may not work for another. The author strongly encourages all readers to:

- Consult with a licensed veterinarian for all health-related questions, concerns, or medical decisions.
- Seek professional animal behaviorist guidance for serious behavioral issues.
- Research and verify any products, breeders, or services mentioned in this book.
- Use their own judgment and adapt suggestions to their specific circumstances.

The author makes no guarantees about the effectiveness of any advice or recommendations provided. References to specific products, brands, breeders, or services are for informational purposes only and do not constitute endorsements.

The author and publisher disclaim any liability for injury, loss, or damage that may result from the use of information in this book. Readers assume full responsibility for their pets' care and well-being.

By reading this book, you acknowledge that you understand these limitations and agree to use the information at your own discretion and risk.

This book represents the author's personal journey with her Bengal cats, Edan and Stormy. It is shared with love for the Bengal community.

Copyright© 2025 Helen Renisch.

All rights reserved.

No part of this book may be reproduced, stored in a retrieval system, or transmitted in any form or by any means—electronic, mechanical, photocopying, recording, or otherwise—without the prior written permission of the author, except as permitted by Australian, United States, or other applicable copyright law.

For permission requests, contact helen@bydezign.pro

Contents

Disclaimer ii

🐾 **PART I: DECIDING & PREPARING** 1

Introduction 1

Chapter 1 Is This Breed Right for You? 11

Chapter 2 Choosing Your Bengal 26

Chapter 3 Bengal-Proofing & Essential Setup 47

Chapter 4 Plant Safety & Your Botanical Detective 68

🐾 **PART II: UNDERSTANIND YOUR BENGAL** 79

Chapter 5 Bengal Behavior Decoded 79

Chapter 6 Meet the Bengal Family 110

🐾 **PART III: DAILY LIFE & CARE** 147

Chapter 7 Feeding Your Bengal 147

Chapter 8 Health Monitoring & Veterinary Care 168

Chapter 9 Litter Box Mastery 187

Chapter 10 Grooming & daily care 199

Chapter 11 Training & Enrichment 214

PART IV: FAMILY LIFE & ADVANCED TOPICS 239

Chapter 12 Socialization, Multi-Pet Homes 239

Chapter 13 Routines for Lifelong Happiness......................261

Chapter 14 Senior Bengal Care 278

Chapter 15 Resources and Shopping Guide...................... 294

Conclusion 338

Acknowledgements... 345

References & Further Reading 346

Author Bio..357

Notes 358

🐾 PART I: DECIDING & PREPARING

Introduction

Welcome to the Jungle from your fearless feline guides, Edan & Stormy!

From the moment you cross the threshold into a home with Bengals, you're stepping into a world of boundless energy, curious antics, and heart-melting affection. This isn't just cat ownership, it's a front-row seat to the wildest, most entertaining show on paws.

I'm Edan, your queen of curiosity and midnight mischief. If there's a height to scale, a cabinet to raid, or a snack to heist, I'm on it. Life with me is a daily adventure, expect the unexpected, and prepare for a companion who'll keep you laughing, guessing, and occasionally rescuing socks from improbable places.

And I'm Stormy, the stealthy ninja of sunbeams and surprise pounces. Whether I'm supervising your every move or testing the limits of household security, I bring a blend of playfulness and purring devotion that's uniquely Bengal.

Together, we're here to turn your home into a playground, your routines into adventures, and your heart into a devoted fan of the spotted life.

Bengal Cats Your Guide for First Time Owners

So, buckle up, dear reader, it's time for the adventure to begin. From us to you, the jungle awaits, and the wild ride starts here.

Pawed and powered up,
Edan & Stormy

INTRODUCTION

Your Free Bengal Resources

This guide includes dozens of practical tools designed specifically for your Bengal journey.

Access all printable checklists, trackers, and planning sheets by scanning the QR code below or accessing the URL www.helenbengalguide.my.canva.site/bonus.

Your Free Resource Library Includes:

- Bengal readiness assessment checklist
- Plant safety quick-reference guide
- Daily routine planning templates
- Behavior troubleshooting tracker
- Training progress charts
- Health monitoring logs
- Shopping comparison worksheets
- Emergency contact templates
- And much more!

BENGAL CATS YOUR GUIDE FOR FIRST TIME OWNERS

Bookmark this page! Throughout the book, you'll find references to these resources. Just come back here, scan the code, and access any tool you need for your Bengal adventure.

Ready to dive in? Edan and Stormy are waiting to guide you through every step of this wild, incredible journey.

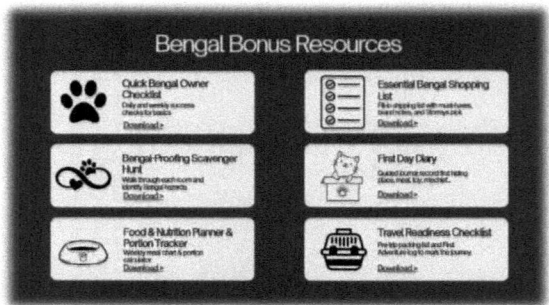

INTRODUCTION

Meet Your Guides

Here are your feline tour guides: Edan, whose curiosity could power a small city, and Stormy, whose stealthy surprises are legendary. Together, they're here to show you that life with a Bengal is less a *quiet afternoon* and more a *"front-row seat to the greatest show on paws."*

"Bengal Live" is your backstage pass to life with the most dynamic, entertaining, and occasionally chaotic housemates you'll ever have. Edan, the queen of curiosity, and Stormy, the surprise attack specialist, are more than guides; they're your co-stars in a never-ending show of feline fun. Welcome to the set; cue the action, hold on to your coffee, and enjoy the ride!

"Edan studies Stormy's next move, considering alerting management. Stormy, meanwhile, is perfectly innocent – probably."

Are Bengals Really Part Wildcat?

Absolutely! Bengals are a hybrid of domestic cats and the Asian leopard cat, developed over generations. Today's Bengals are pure pets, not wild animals. Still, you'll sometimes glimpse their *"jungle"* side in those bold leaps and acrobatic antics. That wild ancestry explains why Edan treats every bookshelf like her personal Mount Everest and why Stormy considers the bathroom sink his private water park; their leopard cat heritage gave them an athlete's energy level and a fascination with heights and water that would make most house cats dizzy. It also means they crave interaction and mental challenges in ways that might surprise you; Edan doesn't just want food, she wants to help choose it, inspect it, and turn every meal into a performance that requires an audience.

The first time I met a Bengal cat, I was unprepared. Edan locked eyes with me as if she already knew all my secrets. From that moment forward, our home was never the same. She brought an energy that made my morning coffee seem redundant. Just as I was getting used to her wild spirit, Stormy arrived, determined to outdo his new sister by chasing invisible bugs and launching surprise attacks from kitchen counters. If you think your life is predictable, try living with two Bengals. You will quickly learn that *"routine"* is just a word in the dictionary.

My name is Helen, and if you are reading this, you are probably either wildly excited or slightly terrified (or maybe a bit of both) about bringing a Bengal cat into your home. I have been there.

INTRODUCTION

I started with one high-voltage kitten and no clue, and now I share my days with two Bengals who treat my house like their personal amusement park.

I wrote this guide for people like you; those who want a friend, not just a pet, and who are ready to laugh, adapt, and occasionally rescue a sock from the jaws of a determined feline. Whether it is two in the morning and your Bengal is yowling at the moon, or you are just wondering how to keep your curtains intact, this book is here to help.

Bengal cats stand apart from all other domestic breeds. Celebrated for their wild beauty and, boundless energy, and unforgettable 'personalities,' they bring a unique mix of adventure, sharp intelligence, and deep affection into any home. Their striking rosettes and marbling can even shimmer with an iridescent glitter in the right light, but their appeal goes far beyond looks. They are comedians, athletes, and loyal friends, ready to turn every day into an adventure.

Inside this guide, you'll discover:

- Real-world stories from my learning curve with Edan and Stormy, from Edan's first escape attempt to Stormy's toilet paper tornado at 3 a.m.
- Complete Bengal-proofing survival guides, cabinet locks that actually work, plant relocation strategies, and why your curtains will never be the same (spoiler: embrace the chaos).

- Daily routine templates for feeding, play sessions, and keeping your sanity when your Bengal decides 5 a.m. is party time.
- Energy management strategies for when your Bengal treats your living room like an obstacle course and your keyboard like a heated cat bed.
- The unvarnished truth about Bengal ownership, from insurance surprises and vet bill realities to why you'll have more photos of your cat than your family.

Edan and Stormy's insider commentary, because who better to explain Bengal logic than the masterminds themselves.

You'll also get access to free printable checklists, planners, and activity sheets to support your Bengal journey by scanning the QR on page 2. (Just open your phone's camera app and point it at the code for instant access!)

Whether you are seeking a loyal companion, a playful partner, or simply want to understand what makes Bengals so special, this guide will help you prepare for the adventure ahead.

Let's embark on this journey together. Your Bengal story starts now.

INTRODUCTION

Edan's Perspective:

"So, you've picked up a book about Bengals? *Wise choice. I'll be conducting my inspection of your home shortly. Expect a thorough evaluation of your climbing furniture, treat selection, and general worthiness as staff. If you think you've prepared adequately, I suppose we'll see. Fair warning: I have very high standards, and your sock drawer is not safe. But suppose you can keep up with my royal scheduling and remember that dinner time is non-negotiable. In that case, we might get along splendidly."*

Stormy's Perspective:

"Hi, I'm Stormy. If you're reading this, you're about to enter a world where every cupboard is a mystery, every sunny spot is a potential nap zone, and every day is a new mission. Don't take life too seriously, unless it's dinner time. Then, please, do take that very seriously."

While I share my experience, you should always consult professionals for health/behavior issues beyond the normal scope. Why Choose a Bengal?

Edan's Welcome:

"Still undecided? Let me introduce you to the wild side!"

Bengal cats aren't just pets; they're bold, beautiful, indoor explorers with a twist of jungle ancestry and buckets of personality. Here's why your home (and heart) will never be the same:

The Bengal Quick List: Top Reasons to Fall in Love

Why You'll Love a Bengal

- **Exquisite Looks:** Glittering rosettes, wild markings, and stunning green eyes; move over, supermodels!
- **Playful Energy:** Every hallway becomes a racetrack, and every shoelace, curtain, or sock turns into spectacular prey.
- **Hugely Affectionate:** Expect surprise cuddles and a shadow that follows you everywhere.
- **Super Smart:** Bengals can learn tricks, play fetch, and (sometimes) even open cupboards.

Chatty Companions: From chirps to chirrups, they'll tell you all about their day, loudly.

- **Dog-like Devotion:** Many Bengals walk on harnesses, greet you at the door, and love a game of fetch.

- **Hypoallergenic:** Some allergy sufferers report fewer symptoms, and their silky coats shed very little.
- **Water Lovers:** Yes, your Bengal may join your bath... or just supervise you from the rim.
- **Entertaining Acrobats:** They leap onto bookcases, vault off the chairs, and star in the daily Bengal Olympics.
- **Family Friendly:** Loyal to their people and often pick a favorite human (don't tell Stormy).

BENGAL CATS YOUR GUIDE FOR FIRST TIME OWNERS

Welcome to Bengal Life: where your houseplants get inspected, keyboard gets sat on, and 'personal space' is just a myth, but every day sparkles with mischief and marvels.

Meet another Bengal ambassador, Bengal glam on duty: poised, alert, and ready to supervise-because every home needs a little jungle royalty and a lot of houseplant security.

Tips for new Bengal owners: Expect the unexpected. Every surface is a runway, every object a potential toy, and every moment, pure entertainment, at least for your cat!

Chapter 1
Is This Breed Right for You?

Welcome to the Jungle, Also Known as Your Living Room.

Picture this: my first day with Edan. I'd spent weeks preparing: cat trees assembled, toys strategically placed, Bengal-proof locks on cabinets. I was ready—or so I thought.

The moment I opened her carrier, my 12-week-old future queen glanced at her new kingdom and made a beeline straight under the lounge suite. For three hours, all I saw were two huge eyes glowing from the shadow, silently calculating, observing, judging my every move. I tried everything—treats, toys, gentle coaxing.

Nothing worked. Just as I surrendered and turned on the TV, she emerged and strutted out like she owned the place all along. Within 10 minutes, she uncovered three escape routes I hadn't noticed, turned my curtains into a climbing wall, and somehow opened the treat drawer I'd sworn was secure. That initial hiding? Not fear, reconnaissance.

What I learned from this experience: Bengal ownership begins with your cat conducting a thorough security audit of their new territory. Your job is to pass inspection while maintaining some semblance of household order.

Just as I was adapting to life with my spotted tornado, Stormy arrived a year later. Where Edan had been calculating even as a kitten, Stormy was pure enthusiasm wrapped in fur. No hiding for him—he burst from his carrier ready to explore, immediately claiming the fluffiest chair as his throne and launching himself onto my shoulder from across the room during my morning coffee.

"As you'll soon discover, living with Edan and Stormy means every day is a new adventure; just wait until you meet your own Bengal tornado!"

The Bengal Reality Check: What You're Really Signing Up For

Before we explore living arrangements and lifestyle compatibility, let's be crystal clear about what Bengal ownership actually means. These aren't your grandmother's lap cats (though they might steal grandma's heart anyway).

The Daily Bengal Experience

Morning (5:30 a.m. - Yes, Really)

Your Bengal alarm clock doesn't have a snooze button. Edan starts with gentle paw taps on my face. If ignored, she escalates to what I call *"the full parkour wake-up call"*—running across my body like I'm just another piece of furniture. Stormy? He prefers the direct approach: sitting on my chest and staring until I crack.

Midday Marathon:

Think working from home means quiet productivity? Your Bengal has other plans. Zoom calls become performance art as your cat inevitably chooses that moment to demonstrate their acrobatic skills. I've lost count of how many colleagues have met Stormy's backside as he walks across my keyboard.

Evening Entertainment:

This is prime Bengal time. While other cats might be satisfied with a simple feather wand, Bengals crave play that challenges their hunter's brain. We're talking puzzle feeders, treat hunts, fetch games (yes, fetch!), and obstacle courses.

Skip this, and your Bengal will create their own entertainment, usually involving your most expensive belongings.

The Time Investment Reality

Here's what your daily Bengal schedule really looks like:

- **Active play:** 30-45 minutes minimum (split between morning and evening)
- **Training/enrichment:** 15-20 minutes (they demand mental challenges)
- **Grooming:** 5-10 minutes (that gorgeous coat needs maintenance)
- **Cleaning:** 15-20 minutes (litter boxes, scattered toys, the occasional "gift")

- **Cuddle/bonding time:** Variable (when they decide, not you)
- **Total daily commitment:** 1.5-2 hours of active engagement, plus passive companionship

"That's 1.5-2 hours daily commitment? Your Bengal will audit this like a time-and-motion expert. Fall behind schedule, and you'll receive a formal complaint delivered via strategic placement of their favorite toy in your coffee mug."

If this time commitment sounds overwhelming right now, that's perfectly fine! Maybe bookmark this page for when life slows down. The Bengals will still be amazing in a few years, and you'll be ready to enjoy every minute.

Living Spaces: Making Any Home a Bengal Friendly

Bengals can thrive in both apartments and houses, provided their need for stimulation is met. Bengals are living room athletes and don't care if their kingdom is a high-rise or a house with a backyard. In a small apartment, **vertical space is your best friend**. Think layered shelves, tall cat trees, and window perches where your Bengal can survey the world (and plot their next move).

The Apartment Bengal Survival Guide:

During my early apartment days with Edan, vertical space quickly became our salvation. Wall-mounted shelves, tall cat trees, and window perches transformed our small space into a Bengal playground.

The Apartment Strategy That Worked for US:

- **Vertical territory expansion:** Floor-to-ceiling cat trees and wall shelves
- **Sound management:** Thick rugs for midnight zoomie zones, rubber mats under cat trees
- **Bathroom vigilance**: Toilet lids down, shower supervision accepted as reality.

One evening, Edan showcased her vertical genius by transforming my apartment's bare wall into a racetrack—leaping from mounted shelf to shelf, then perching atop the fridge like a spotty crowning jewel. She barely used my living room's footprint, but her aerial antics made the space feel limitless.

Success Story:

When Jay moved into a city apartment, he feared his tiny space could never satisfy Bengal's energy. He installed shelves, a floor-to-ceiling cat tree, and a window hammock. Within weeks, his Bengal, Saffron, had established her own *"sky circuit"* around the flat. Jay's friends were amazed—not just at Saffron's energy, but at how content she was, surveying the world from her sky-high perches. Now, Jay laughs, *"It's not a small apartment. It's a Bengal playground—and we live here together quite happily."*

House Living: Managing Your Mini Leopard's Territory

A house offers more space, but Bengals will use EVERY inch. They don't just live in your home; they explore, investigate, and establish territorial claims.

What I learned managing Edan and Stormy in a larger space:

- Different floors become different territories to patrol.
- Multiple litter boxes and feeding stations prevent resource competition.
- Baby gates don't work (they'll jump or climb).
- Secure outdoor access requires supervision or Catios, never unsupervised roaming.

Success Story:

Mia was convinced a Bengal would never fit into her busy city life. After months of research, she adopted Apollo, a rescued Bengal with a penchant for hiding under beds. With some vertical spaces and interactive toys, Apollo gradually gained confidence. Now, Mia describes him as her *"roommate, alarm clock, and entertainment director."* Apollo's favorite pastime? Watching the world from his window hammock, occasionally punctuating his observations with a dramatic flying leap, just to keep Mia on her toes.

CHAPTER 1
IS THIS BREED RIGHT FOR YOU?

Edan's Perspective:

"Apartments are just vertical playgrounds waiting to happen. My record? Floor to ceiling in 3.2 seconds. The key is training your human to think three-dimensionally."

Stormy's Perspective:

"Houses are like multiple apartments stacked together! More rooms, more places to hide toys and surprise humans. My favorite game? Racing from basement to attic in record time."

Storm may be pint-sized, but those eyes say he's already plotting world (or at least living room) domination!

CHAPTER 1
IS THIS BREED RIGHT FOR YOU?

Financial Reality Check

Let's talk money, because Bengals aren't budget pets:

Year One Investment

Initial Investment: $2000-$5000 AUD

- Bengal kitten from reputable breeder: $1,500-$4,000 (approx. $975–$2,600 USD).
- Setup & Supplies: $500-$1,000 (approx. $325–$650 USD).
- First-year vet care: $500-$800 (approx. $325–$520 USD).

Annual Ongoing Costs: $1600-$3000 AUD

- Quality food: $600-$1,000 (approx. $390–$650 USD).
- Healthcare: $300-$500 (approx. $195–$325 USD).
- Litter: $200-$400 (approx. $130–$260 USD).
- Enrichment & toys: $200-$500 (approx. $130–$325 USD).
- Insurance: $300-$600 (approx. $195–$390 USD).

Emergency Fund: Keep $2,000-$5,000 AUD (approx. $1,300–$3,250 USD) available. Bengals are athletic and curious, sometimes too curious for their own good.

"Emergency fund reality: Bengals have an uncanny ability to schedule their most expensive adventures for the exact moment your bank account feels comfortable. It's like they have a direct line to your financial stress levels."

Note: US dollar equivalents are approximate, calculated at 1 AUD = 0.65 USD as of November 2025. Exchange rates may change over time.

These numbers are based on my actual experience with Edan and Stormy over several years. Your costs may vary, but budget realistically. Quality care is expensive but necessary.

Top 5 Rookie Mistakes That I Made So You Don't Have To

1. "My Bengal Doesn't Need That Much Exercise"

The Lesson: Watch your curtains become their gym equipment. A tired Bengal is a good Bengal. An energetic Bengal is a home decorator's nightmare. I learned this when Edan decided the living room drapes were perfect for her morning parkour routine.

2. "This Plant Looks Nice Here"

The Reality: Your Bengal sees a salad bar. Research every plant before bringing it home. Edan once ate half a (thankfully non-toxic) fern just to prove she could reach it.

3. "I Don't Need to Bengal-Proof Everything"

Famous Last Words: Stormy learned to open lever door handles at six months. Nothing is truly Bengal-proof, but you can at least make them work for their mischief.

4. "My Bengal Will Be Fine Alone All Day"

The Consequence: Return home to find they've redecorated extensively. With toilet paper. Everywhere! Bengals need interaction and mental stimulation.

5. "They'll Grow Out of It"

The Truth: Bengals don't grow out of anything; they grow INTO it. That cute kitten climbing habit becomes adult cat parkour. The playful swatting becomes precision pouncing. Plan for the Bengal they'll become, not just the kitten they are.

Each of these mistakes taught me something valuable about Bengal ownership. Consider them tuition payments in my Bengal education.

Activity: Check off mistakes you've already learned from. Add your own discoveries below. Share your funniest Bengal mistake on social media with #BengalRookieMoment.

The Bengal Promise: What You Give vs. What You Get

- **What You Give:** Time, energy, money, patience, creativity, and love (lots of love).
- **What You Get:** A comedian, companion, bed warmer, and tornado who may yowl at 3 a.m., but will also greet you at the door like you've been gone for years, entertain you daily with acrobatics, and purr you to sleep when you need it most.

Decision Time: Your Bengal Readiness Action Plan

This Week:

- Visit a Bengal breeder or rescue in person.
- Join an online Bengal community to observe daily reality.
- Calculate your actual Bengal budget (don't forget the emergency fund).
- Start practicing 5:30 a.m. wake-ups (seriously).

CHAPTER 1
IS THIS BREED RIGHT FOR YOU?

This Month:

- Spend extended time with adult Bengals (energy levels, not just kitten cuteness).
- Begin Bengal-proofing your space.
- Research Bengal-savvy veterinarians in your area.
- Get household member buy-in (everyone needs to be on board).

Before You Commit:

- Have your emergency fund established.
- Arrange backup care for travel or illness.
- Accept that life as you know it changes here.
- Embrace the adventure mentality.

Edan's Perspective:

"Honestly, we're not easy. We're demanding, dramatic, and occasionally destructive. But if you want a cat who is just furniture, get a stuffed animal. If you want a partner in crime, a comedian, an athlete, and a cuddle bug rolled into one spectacular spotted package—welcome to the Bengal club. Just hide your good shoes. And that reconnaissance mission under the couch? I had you figured out in three hours flat."

Stormy's Perspective:

"The truth is, you don't really choose a Bengal. We choose you. We pick the humans who can handle our energy, appreciate our intelligence, and laugh when we inevitably do something ridiculous at 2 a.m. If you're reading this and smiling instead of running away, you're probably our kind of people. See you at 5:30 a.m. for our first play session!"

Final Thoughts

Choosing a Bengal isn't about perfection; it's about compatibility. If you're looking for adventure, intelligence, loyalty, entertainment, and a true partnership with a cat that has opinions about everything, then congratulations. You're ready to join the wonderful, wild world of Bengal ownership.

These mini leopards will challenge every assumption you have about cats, push your patience, test your creativity, and somehow steal your heart in the process. But they'll also teach you that the best relationships, whether human or feline, are built on mutual respect, shared adventure, and the ability to find joy in the unexpected.

Ready to take the plunge? Let's move on to finding your perfect Bengal companion.

Chapter 2
Choosing Your Bengal

Let me begin with a confession: I thought I was bringing home a cat. What I actually brought home was a furry whirlwind with the curiosity of Indiana Jones, the energy of a toddler at a trampoline park, and the unwavering belief that every household rule was merely a *suggestion* open for *negotiation*. Edan arrived, surveyed her new kingdom with those glowing, green eyes, and immediately set about conducting what I can only describe as an elaborate security audit of the premises—starting with a thorough investigation of the lounge suite's underbelly and culminating in a dramatic conquest of the curtain rails.

What I learned from this experience: Bengal ownership isn't just about bringing a pet home; it's about welcoming a partner in adventure who may occasionally redistribute your belongings for *"quality improvement purposes."*

CHAPTER 2
CHOOSING YOUR BENGAL

Understanding Bengal Personality: Beyond the Spotted Coat

While their wild rosettes and glittering coats grab attention, what truly defines Bengals is their exceptional intelligence paired with the energy of an Olympic athlete. In my experience with Edan and Stormy, these cats are less like traditional house pets and more like tiny, spotted personal trainers who've appointed themselves directors of household entertainment.

What This Actually Means in Daily Life:

- **High Energy = Creative Solutions Required**
  When Edan's not scaling bookshelves, Stormy's perfecting his flying leap technique from the kitchen counter. Traditional *"cat toys"* lasted about a week before they decided household items offered better challenges.

- **Intelligence = Constant Problem-Solving.**
  Edan once figured out how to open a supposedly Bengal-proof cabinet lock. Stormy learned to operate door handles at six months. These aren't party tricks; they're daily reminders that you're living with cats who consider puzzles a form of entertainment.

- **Social Nature = You Have a Shadow (Or Two)** Bengals don't just want to be near you; they want to participate in your activities. Expect supervising humans to become their full-time occupation, from bathroom visits to Zoom meetings.

Every Bengal is unique, but these core traits come standard. What varies is how each Bengal expresses their particular brand of genius.

The Softer Side: When Wild Cats Want Cuddles

Despite their flair for drama and athletic feats, Bengals are surprisingly world-class cuddlers. Edan can shift from Zoom-rocket to Zen master in seconds, melting onto my lap mid-deadline and purring loud enough to make my coffee ripple.

The Reality of Bengal Snuggles: They're not lap cats in the traditional sense—they're lap cats on their own terms. When Stormy decides it's cuddle time, he'll sprawl across whatever you're doing with the confidence of someone who's never been told *"not now."* The warmth, weight, and purring create an instant stress-relief session, assuming you can surrender control of your schedule to feline priorities.

CHAPTER 2
CHOOSING YOUR BENGAL

Behold the mighty Bengal: one-part ancient pharaoh, one part freshly baked loaf. The royal decree? Your lap is now the kingdom's official napping throne!

Tips for Encouraging Cuddle Sessions (From My Experience)

- **Warmth wins every time**, sunny spots and heated laps are irresistible.
- **Post-play wind-down time** often leads to snuggle opportunities.
- **Soft blankets** seem to trigger their inner comfort-seekers.
- **Don't force it**, Bengal cuddles are gifts, not obligations.

What surprised me most: These supposedly *"wild"* cats often seek out quiet companionship just as much as active play. Learning to recognize and appreciate both sides has deepened our relationship immeasurably.

Activity: Bengal Snuggle Tracker

Keep a journal for a week: note when and where your Bengal chooses to cuddle. Is it morning, after meals, or during your favorite show? Compare notes with other Bengal owners and see who has the biggest lap cat!

The Cat-Dog Phenomenon: When Your Cat Has Canine Ambitions

My husband jokes that we accidentally brought home cats running on *"dog software,"* and honestly, he's not wrong. Edan comes when called (unless she's conducting important curtain research), and Stormy greets visitors at the door like a **golden retriever in a spotted suit.**

CHAPTER 2
CHOOSING YOUR BENGAL

"Edan and Stormy demonstrate the rare art of 'recharge cuddles,' required when you spend most of your day operating on dog-level enthusiasm and cat-level genius. Note: This display of peace is 100% genuine, but the quiet will be short-lived. Enjoy the calm, until the next game of fetch begins."

Bengal "Dog Behaviors" I've Observed:

Following you from room to room for no apparent reason:

- Supervising all household activities with keen interest.
- Playing fetch with surprising enthusiasm (Stormy's record: **thirteen perfect paper-ball returns).**
- Greeting guests with a tail-up excitement.
- *"Helping"* with dinner by conducting thorough quality control taste tests.

This isn't universal; every Bengal has their own personality mix. But if you've always wanted a pet that combines feline independence with canine devotion, Bengals often deliver both.

Lifestyle Reality Check: Are You Ready for Bengal Life?

Before you fully lose yourself in those hypnotic rosettes, let's have an honest talk about what Bengal ownership actually involves. This isn't about discouraging you; it's about setting realistic expectations so you can succeed.

The Daily Bengal Commitment (What I Wish Someone Had Told Me):

- **40+ minutes of active** play daily (not optional, think of it as Bengal exercise requirements).

- **Mental Workout** (puzzle feeders, rotating toys, new experiences)
- **Flexibility exceptions** (Bengals have strong opinions about interior design).
- **Energy for interactive engagement** (these cats want to participate in your life, not just observe it).
- **Sense of humor about chaos** (things will get moved, opened, and occasionally redecorated).

Questions to Ask Yourself:

- Can you handle a pet who treats every closed door as a personal challenge?
- Are you prepared for a cat who wants to *"help"* with everything you do?
- Can you laugh when your carefully planned day gets interrupted by feline priorities?
- Do you have backup plans for when your Bengal outsmarts your Bengal-proofing?

If you answered yes while smiling, you might be ready for Bengal ownership. If you answered yes while feeling slightly terrified, that's also normal; most of us started there.

Finding Your Bengal: The Search Strategy

Breeders vs. Rescues: Both Have Stories to Tell

- **Reputable Breeders:** Offer predictability: You'll know your kitten's health history, meet the parents, and often receive a well-socialized, confident cat. The best breeders become lifelong resources, answering questions and providing support long after you take your Bengal home.
- **Rescue Bengals:** Offer second chances: These cats may have mysterious pasts, but they also bring grateful hearts and proven resilience. Many rescue Bengals are adults, so you'll see their full personalities instead of guessing how a kitten might develop.

From my experience, the key isn't where you find your Bengal but who you get them from. Seek ethical people who put cat welfare above profit. Good breeders and good rescues both exist—the trick is recognizing them.

Activity: Decision-Making Self-Check

List your *"must-haves"* and **deal-breakers**: kitten or adult, predictable or mysterious? This self-check keeps your heart and logic aligned, vital when your emotions meet those irresistible spots.

CHAPTER 2
CHOOSING YOUR BENGAL

Testimonial from a Rescue Bengal Mum:

"The day we brought Leo home, he marched out of his carrier, sniffed every corner, and immediately claimed the sunniest windowsill as his throne. Within an hour, he was purring in my lap as if he'd always belonged. There's a special magic in that first meeting, a sense that you're not just adopting a cat but welcoming a bold new friend into your story."

Testimonials Matter:

Stories like Leo's prove that rescue Bengals often adapt with astonishing grace, full of courage, affection, and gratitude for their new chapter.

Kitten vs. Adult: What to Expect

Bringing a Bengal cat home, whether a bouncy kitten or a wise adult, is an adventure, but the first days look a little different! Here's what to expect:

Kitten vs. Adult: What to Expect

	Kitten Bengal	Adult Bengal
Energy	Nonstop zoomies, playful pounces, and sudden naps.	Curious but more measured; explores at their own pace.
Confidence	May hide, then bounce out and investigate everything.	May be cautious or bold, often checks out the room, then claims a spot.
Eating	Eats often, sometimes messily; may need encouragement.	Eats larger meals, may be picky or "affection eater."
Litter Box	Needs reminders and easy access; accidents possible.	Usually litter trained but may need time to adjust to new box/location.
Bonding	Seeks comfort, loves gentle petting, quick to purr.	May take longer to warm up; enjoys quiet company, slow blinks, or lap time.
Sleep	Catnaps everywhere, laundry baskets, under beds, on your pillow.	Chooses a favorite nap spot; less likely to hide once settled.
Mischief	Climbing, chewing, exploring every nook.	Investigates new spaces, but (usually) with more dignity.

Tip: Kittens need more supervision and reassurance, while adults may crave routine and gentle introductions. Both will capture your heart in their unique ways!

Breeder Red Flags vs. Green Lights

Red Flags That Should Send You Running:

- Refusing home visits or video calls.
- Dodging questions about health testing or socialization.
- Pressure for immediate payment or *"hold fees."*
- No health guarantees or return policies.
- Multiple litters available at all times (suggests a puppy mill approach).

Green Lights That Suggest Quality:

- Welcomes questions and provides detailed answers.
- Shows you where cats live and socialize.
- Provides health testing results for breeding cats.
- Offers ongoing support and stays in touch.
- Has waiting lists (good breeders aren't always available immediately).

The First Meeting: What to Look For

When you finally meet potential Bengals, look for confidence, curiosity, and social engagement rather than just focusing on coat patterns. A healthy Bengal kitten should greet you with interest, play with enthusiasm, and show no signs of hiding or fear.

Health Indicators I Learned to Watch For:

- Bright, clear eyes and clean ears.
- Soft, shiny coat with no bald patches.
- Playful curiosity about new people and environments.
- Clean litter box habits.
- Appropriate weight for age.

Remember: you're not just choosing a cat; you're choosing a personality to share your home with for the next 12-18 years. Take time to observe how potential Bengals interact with people, other cats, and their environment.

CHAPTER 2
CHOOSING YOUR BENGAL

Trust your instincts. If something feels off, keep looking

The Paperwork Trail: Protecting Your Investment

Essential Documents You Should Receive:

- Complete health records, including vaccinations.
- Microchip information and registration details.
- Pedigree papers (if from a breeder).
- Clear contracts with health guarantees.
- Emergency contact information for the breeder/rescue.

Metanoia Bengal Sire - Stormy's Dad "When you're this handsome, even rolling in the grass turns into a full-blown photo shoot!"

Pro Tip from Experience:

When you take your cat home, start a Bengal Binder, physical or digital, the moment you bring your cat home. You will be surprised how much you will use it during vet visits, travel, or emergencies. Having it all under one roof will save you stress and is what will make you feel like the organized pet parent you want to become.

First 48 Hours: The Adjustment Period

Those first hours can define your relationship. Whether your Bengal hides under furniture for reconnaissance (like Edan) or immediately begins exploring with confident determination (Stormy's trademark), follow their lead; patience builds trust faster than reassurance ever could.

CHAPTER 2
CHOOSING YOUR BENGAL

What Worked for Us:

- Set up a quiet *"base camp"* with all essentials in one room.
- Sit nearby, reading or working, letting curiosity naturally overcome caution.
- Offer treats and gentle conversation without forcing interaction.
- Document the milestones, first meal, first toy interaction, and first purr.

When to Worry vs. When to Wait:

- Not eating after 24 hours = vet call.
- Hiding and observing for a day or two = normal adjustment.
- Extreme lethargy or breathing issues = immediate vet attention.
- Cautious exploration and gradual confidence building = perfect progress.

Naming Your Bengal: The Identity Decision

Naming your Bengal might seem simple until you realize how much you'll be using it. Bengals often come when called (when it suits them), so pick something you won't mind saying repeatedly.

What Works Well:

- Two-syllable names (easier for cats to recognize).
- Names that reflect personality or appearance.
- Names you can say with authority when needed ("Edan, get off the counter!").

Edan's Name Story: When I learned *"Edan"* means *"little arrow"* in some traditions, it felt perfect for a kitten with arrow-shaped rosettes and a personality that goes straight for whatever catches her interest. The name fit her looks and her direct approach to life; no regrets there.

Every Bengal develops into their name differently. Choose something that feels right to you; they'll make it their own regardless.

Activity: Name Brainstorm

List names inspired by looks, personality, and favorites. Try them out, do any make you smile or get a Bengal head-tilt?

Be Unique, Be You:

Don't hold back on creativity. The names of great Bengals are often mythological (Athena, Apollo), of the natural world (River, Saffron, Jade), or even the favorites of the books and movies (Mowgli, Loki, Nala). Name something that will make you smile; it is your first adventure together.

Test It Out:

Say the name aloud a few times, during play, feeding, or cuddle breaks. If your Bengal responds to the name or it makes you smile, you've likely found the perfect fit.

Popular Bengal Names:

- **Girls:** Amber, Luna, Nala, Saffron, Marble, Athena, Willow, Ember, Sasha, Zara.
- **Boys:** Leo, Rajah, Hunter, Onyx, Storm, Loki, Maverick, Blitz, Zeus.
- **Unisex:** River, Shadow, Jazz, Tiger, Pepper, Jade, Dash, Cheetah.

Ultimately, the name you choose for your Bengal marks the beginning of your adventure together. Choose one that celebrates their beauty, personality, and the wild spirit that makes this breed so unforgettable

Edan's Name: My Little Arrow and Fiery Spirit.

Celebration vs. Preparation: The Balance

Welcoming a Bengal is exciting, but success comes from balancing enthusiasm with practical preparation. The most important thing you can do is to approach Bengal ownership with realistic expectations, a sense of humor, and genuine appreciation for their unique personalities.

Activity: Bengal Readiness Self-Assessment

Before making your final decision, honestly evaluate:

- Your energy level for daily interactive play.
- Your tolerance for household chaos and redecoration.
- Your budget for quality food, vet care, and emergency funds.
- Your lifestyle flexibility for Bengal-centered scheduling.
- Your commitment to long-term care through all life stages.

Edan's Name: Her eyes say it all. My Little Arrow and Fiery Spirit.

Chapter 2
Choosing Your Bengal

Edan's Perspective:

"So, you're thinking about joining my species as a servant? Wise choice. I'll need references, a detailed schedule of treat deliveries, and proof that you understand my position as household royalty. If you pass the inspection, I might allow you to live in my house. Fair warning: I have very high standards and excellent memory for lapses in service."

Stormy's Perspective:

"New humans always seem nervous during the interview process. Relax—we're pretty easygoing as long as you remember who's really in charge. I require comfortable furniture, regular entertainment, and someone who appreciates the finer points of slow-motion stretching. If you can handle that, we'll get along just fine."

Final Thoughts

Choosing a Bengal isn't just about finding the right cat; it's about finding the right partnership. Whether you choose a confident kitten from a breeder or open your heart to a rescue Bengal with their own history, what matters most is the commitment to understand, appreciate, and adapt to their unique needs.

In my experience, the best Bengal matches happen when humans embrace the adventure rather than trying to control it. These cats will change your routine, challenge your assumptions, and occasionally redecorate your home. In return, they'll provide entertainment, affection, and daily reminders that life is better with a sense of humor.

The decision to bring a Bengal home marks the beginning of a relationship unlike any other pet ownership experience. Take your time, ask questions, trust your instincts, and prepare for a journey that's equal parts challenging and rewarding.

Remember: Every Bengal has its own personality, preferences, and preferred methods of household management. Your job isn't to change them, it's to create an environment where their natural Bengal qualities can flourish safely and happily.

Chapter 3
Bengal-Proofing & Essential Setup

Setting the Stage for a Feline Tornado

Every Bengal owner's journey begins with optimism, a shopping list, and the naive belief that you can Bengal-proof anything. When I prepared for Edan's arrival, I spent weeks researching, buying locks, and moving breakables. I was so

"Edan, demonstrating the ancient art of 'I bet you thought I couldn't get up here.'"

proud of my thoroughness until she promptly found the one plant I had forgotten to relocate and wore it as a fashionable, leafy hat while giving me a look that clearly said, 'Amateur.'

In my experience, Bengal-proofing is less about achieving perfection and more about staying one step ahead of a furry Einstein with boundary issues. Here's what I learned through trial, error, and several frantic Google searches...

Bengal-Proofing Your Home: The Real Game Begins

Bengals aren't just cats; they're furry escape artists, acrobats, and amateur demolition experts with Ph.D.-level problem-solving skills. Preparing your home means thinking like a Bengal: curious, clever, and convinced that every closed door is a personal challenge.

"The "Stormy Learned to Open This Hall of Fame features items like door handles and treat cupboards. His top achievement is opening a supposedly 'Bengal-proof' latch while holding eye contact, as if to say, 'Challenge accepted and demolished.'"

CHAPTER 3
BENGAL-PROOFING & ESSENTIAL SETUP

Master Checklist: Bengal-Proofing Essentials

The *"Stormy Learned to Open This"* List

Bengal-Proof Your Home:

- Store breakables in secure cabinets, not on open shelves (Stormy's paws have a surprisingly long reach).
- Install childproof latches on cupboards, and yes, they work on Bengal-proof as well.
- Close toilet lids unless you enjoy wet paw prints on every surface.
- Hide cords, headphones, and anything that dangles (Edan considers these interactive toys).
- Secure or move houseplants (more on this botanical journey below).

Vertical Highway Planning:

- Invest in tall, sturdy cat trees, emphasize sturdiness (flimsy furniture is Bengal kryptonite).
- Install wall-mounted shelves for safe (cat highways).
- Create window perches for professional sun-soaking and birdwatching duties.
- Designate a cozy *"safe zone"* for downtime, like a basket, box, or any spot with a blanket for comfort. My Favorite Tip: Place scratching posts near favorite nap zones.

What I wish someone had told me: If you think you've Bengal-proofed everything, you've probably missed something. That's not failure, that's Bengal ownership. The goal is damage control, not perfection.

The Bengal Owner's Golden Rule:

For a happy Bengal (and a safe, undamaged house), create your climbing kingdom, fill it with plenty of tempting toys, and keep playtime energetic. All the top Bengal-proofing tips, vertical upgrades, and play routines are gathered in our *"Setting Up for Success"* chapter. Throughout the book, you'll see reminders to revisit whenever you're exploring new rooms, reaching age milestones, or managing holiday chaos.

Check here first, then add new specifics only when there's a twist or seasonal change; your sanity (and your furniture) will thank you!

Cat Trees & Vertical Play		
Brand/Model	**Features**	**Notes**
Mau Lifestyle	Modern, sturdy, real wood	Blends with home décor
Vesper	Modular, replaceable parts	Soft memory foam cushions
Tuft + Paw	Designer cat furniture	Premium, high-end look
Catkea	Budget-friendly, easy to assemble	Good starter option

CHAPTER 3
BENGAL-PROOFING & ESSENTIAL SETUP

Activity: Design Your Cat's Vertical Playground

- Sketch your living room and plan where to add cat trees, shelves, or window perches.
- List three ways to change the setup each month for enrichment.

Cat Trees & Vertical Play

"If you're looking for durable cat trees or climbing shelves, here are a few brands Bengal owners often mention. These are just starting points; explore and find what works best for your space and your cat's style."

The Cat Door Chronicles

Installing a cat door in my bedroom door might seem like a luxury. Still, for Bengal owners, it's a practical stroke of genius. This smart little access point keeps the warmth inside on cold nights while letting Edan and Stormy come and go as they please, with no midnight yowling at the door needed. The best part? These small doors can open and close easily, enabling the cats to maintain their independence while I enjoy my sleep and keep my heating costs low. It's a win-win for both humans and Bengals, proof that sometimes, the smallest doors make the biggest difference.

Stormy makes his grand entrance because every Bengal deserves their own VIP door service!

CHAPTER 3
BENGAL-PROOFING & ESSENTIAL SETUP

Essential Bengal Shopping List

Before your Bengal arrives, stock up on the essentials. For example, make sure you have a scratching post ready before the new couch arrives.

Must-Haves

- Litter box (with high sides). We will discuss litter boxes in Chapter 9: Litter Box Mastery.
- Multiple sturdy scratching posts.
- Food and water bowls (heavy, tip-proof).
- Interactive toys.
- Soft beds.
- Grooming tools.

Stormy takes his puzzle toys seriously. Bengal brains need daily workouts!

What to Skip

- Plastic bowls and litter boxes.
- Flimsy cat trees or posts.
- Toys with small parts that could be swallowed.
- Scented litter (as many Bengals are picky about smells).

Activity: Shopping List Challenge

- Print out the checklist and bring it with you to the store, or use it online.
- Check off each item as you go; bonus points for finding a toy your Bengal actually prefers over the box it came in.

Essential Bengal Shopping: Learning from My Mistakes

Before Edan arrived, I thought regular cat supplies would suffice. I was adorably mistaken. Here's what truly works for the Bengals, based on costly trial and error.

Bengals are lively and sometimes a bit theatrical about their meals and drinks. The right bowls can make a huge difference.

CHAPTER 3
BENGAL-PROOFING & ESSENTIAL SETUP

Food and Water Bowls: The "Stormy Skated This Across the Kitchen" Edition What Works (Hard-Learned lessons):

- Heavy, tip-proof bowls (lightweight bowls turn into hockey pucks).
- Ceramic or stainless steel (easy to clean and bacteria-resistant).
- Wide and shallow (prevents whisker fatigue, although I'm not sure Edan experiences this issue).
- Cats can be fussy about water bowls, so expect some trial and error to find one your Bengal will drink from. (Stormy loves running water, it is fresher, more appealing, and encourages him to drink more).

What Doesn't Work (Expensive Mistakes):

- Plastic bowls (they scratch easily and can cause chin acne).
- Anything lightweight (see Stormy's bowl-skating adventure).
- Fancy fountains with too many parts (unless you love cleaning them daily).

Every Bengal is unique, but these options worked in our chaotic home. Your Bengal might have very different preferences-they're excellent at expressing their opinions.

Food & Water Bowls

"To make shopping easier, here are some bowl brands and types that other Bengal owners use. Feel free to compare their features and find what fits your Bengal's needs and your home."

Food & Water Bowls		
Brand / Model	**Features**	**Notes**
Catit	Stainless steel, whisker-friendly	Easy to clean, affordable
Pioneer Pet	Ceramic, wide shallow bowls	Prevents whisker fatigue
PetFusion	Non-slip, modern design	Heavy, hard to tip over
PetSafe Drinkwell	Water fountain, filtered	Encourages hydration

Chapter 3
Bengal-Proofing & Essential Setup

The First Day: Reality Meets Preparation

When Edan first arrived, I thought I had everything perfectly arranged. She looked at my carefully planned setup and quickly showed me that Bengal cats don't read human instruction manuals. Stormy, on the other hand, immediately found the treat cupboard and staged a one-cat heist.

What to Actually Expect:

- Your Bengal will discover the hiding spot you didn't realize existed.
- They'll prefer the box that came with the toys over the expensive toys.
- Every surface will be checked for climbing potential.
- Your detailed plans will only serve as... guidelines at best.

First Day Success Tips (Learned from Experience):

- Set up a quiet *"base camp"* with essentials.
- Let your Bengal lead the exploration pace.
- Make sure doors and windows are locked (trust me on this).
- Have your camera ready, you'll want to remember this chaos.

The key is flexibility. Your Bengal has its own agenda, and your job is to keep up while keeping everyone safe. "Day one: blending in with the dust bunnies. Mission accomplished."

Activity: First Day Diary

- Write down your Bengal's first hiding spot, first meal, and first zoomie.
- Take a photo to remember the moment (and compare it to future chaos).

CHAPTER 3
BENGAL-PROOFING & ESSENTIAL SETUP

Introducing the Family: Humans, Pets, and the Vacuum Cleaner

Bengal cats are social but can be cautious around unfamiliar people and settings. Introduce new family members gradually and remember that the vacuum cleaner may scare them.

- Start with scent exchanges.
- Supervise first meetings and keep them short and positive.
- Reward calm behavior.
- For dogs, keep them on a leash at first.
- For other cats, use a baby gate or a cracked door.

BENGAL CATS YOUR GUIDE FOR FIRST TIME OWNERS

Metanoia Hunter with his pet Labrador, "Negotiations are underway. The Treaty of Living Room is pending."

Activity: Meet-and-Greet Log

- Note each family member's first interaction with your Bengal.
- Record reactions, both feline and human!

CHAPTER 3
BENGAL-PROOFING & ESSENTIAL SETUP

Traveling with Your Bengal

Note: This section covers the basics of Bengal travel. For detailed travel planning, many owners find success with online pet travel resources and airline guidelines. However, every Bengal's travel tolerance varies.

With a little preparation and a sense of humor, you'll help your Bengal feel safe and even enjoy the adventure. Here's how to make each trip smoother, safer, and more enjoyable. Since you'll need to get your Bengal home safely and will likely face vet visits, here are the travel basics that worked for us.

Choosing the Right Carrier

The Edan and Stormy Travel Reality: For our yearly vet visits, I learned that these two need to travel together; separation anxiety kicks in when they can't see each other during stressful situations. We use a large, sturdy carrier that comfortably fits both cats, with familiar blankets for security and enough space for Stormy's dramatic stretching while Edan supervises from her preferred corner. The shared carrier actually reduces their stress because they can provide mutual moral support during the journey.

What This Taught Me About Multi-Bengal Travel:

- Bonded cats often feel more secure traveling together than separately.
- A larger single carrier can work better than two individual carriers for short trips.
- Both cats settle faster when they can see and smell their companion.
- Familiar scents (their shared blankets) matter more than individual carrier preferences.

This setup might not work for every multi-cat household, but for Edan and Stormy, having each other during vet visits has made the experience much easier for everyone involved.

Basic Carrier Guidelines (From Our Experience):

- Hard carriers for longer trips or escape artists.
- Soft carriers for vet visits and calm travelers.
- Always secure them with seatbelts in cars.
- Familiar scents make everything better.

Each Bengal has unique travel preferences. Begin with short trips to determine what suits your specific cat.

Chapter 3
Bengal-Proofing & Essential Setup

Table: Carrier Types & When to Use from our experience

Cat Carrier Types & When to Use

Carrier Type	Best For	Legal Notes / Travel Tips
Soft Carrier	Car trips, vet visits	Legal for cars/public transport, not cargo air
Hard Carrier	Air travel, long trips	Required for cargo air, safest for strong cats

Stormy's First Ride:

Edan's first car trip was easy; she sprawled out, watched the world go by, and only meowed when we hit a bump. Stormy, on the other hand, sang the song of his people the entire way home. Every Bengal is different, so be ready for anything!

Traveling with your Bengal doesn't have to be stressful. With the right carrier, some prep, and a sense of humor, you'll both arrive safe, sound, and maybe even a little closer. Whether your Bengal is an Edan (laid back) Stormy (vocal and dramatic), every trip is another chapter in your adventure together.

"You said 'adventure'; this is not what I had in mind."

Common First-Week Surprises (Nobody Warned Me About These)

- **The "Midnight Zoomies" Discovery:** Sleep becomes optional when Edan decides that 3 a.m. is prime raceway time. This is normal Bengal behavior, not a personal attack on your sleep schedule.
- **The "Everything is Interactive" Revelation:** Bengals don't distinguish between toys and household items. Your coffee mug, keyboard, and favorite pen are all fair game for quality testing.

CHAPTER 3
BENGAL-PROOFING & ESSENTIAL SETUP

- **The "Sudden Affection Attacks":** When you think you understand your Bengal's routine, they'll decide your laptop is the perfect cuddle spot during important video calls.
- **The Unexpected Hiding Spots:** Stormy disappeared for hours, only to be found snoozing in a laundry basket.

These aren't problems to fix; they're Bengal features to adapt to. Welcome the chaos; resistance is useless.

"If I fits, I naps. Laundry day is now a team sport."

65

Activity: Bengal Bingo

Create a bingo card with common Bengal antics:

- Curtain climbing ✓
- Midnight zoomies ✓
- Food theft attempt ✓
- Surprise cuddle ambush ✓
- Plant investigation ✓

Mark off each behavior as you see it. Reward yourself after five in a row, you've officially been initiated into Bengal ownership!

Edan's Perspective:

"You think you've Bengal-proofed everything? How charming. I'll be conducting my inspection soon, and I expect to find at least three security vulnerabilities. If you've hidden the treats too well, I see that as a personal challenge. Fair warning: I have all day and excellent problem-solving skills."

Stormy's Perspective:

"New home, new rules, new opportunities for mischief. I'll take my time exploring, every cupboard, every shelf, every cozy corner needs proper investigation. The toilet paper situation requires immediate attention, and that curtain looks suspiciously climbable. Welcome to Team Bengal; hope you packed your sense of humor."

CHAPTER 3
BENGAL-PROOFING & ESSENTIAL SETUP

Final Thoughts

Bengal-proofing isn't a one-time task; it's an ongoing process of balancing your desire for a safe home with your Bengal's need to explore. The goal isn't to eliminate all Bengal mischief (which is impossible) but to create a secure environment where their natural behaviors won't result in emergency vet visits or expensive replacements.

Remember: What worked perfectly for Edan and Stormy might not work for your Bengal. Every cat has its own personality, preferences, and favorite ways of creating household chaos. The key is staying adaptable, maintaining your sense of humor, and always having backup plans for your backup plans.

Some days you'll feel like a zookeeper, and other days like a detective solving the mystery of the missing hair comb. Most days, you'll just marvel at sharing your home with such intelligent, entertaining, and rarely exhausting companions.

Your Bengal will surprise you. Embrace the chaos, laugh at the antics, and remember, every day with a Bengal is a new adventure.

"Once you've secured the obvious hazards like breakables and escape routes, there's one category of household items that requires special attention: your plants. What seems like harmless greenery to humans can pose serious risks to curious Bengal explorers."

Chapter 4
Plant Safety & Your Botanical Detective

The Great Plant Safety Adventure

A Comprehensive Guide from Edan's Botanical Experiments

Living with Bengals means every houseplant becomes a potential science experiment. Edan's approach to plant identification involves thorough taste-testing, while Stormy prefers the archaeological method of digging up roots for closer inspection.

Why This Section Is So Long: After Edan's first plant encounter (thankfully non-toxic but costly), I became obsessed with plant safety. What started as basic research evolved into a detailed database because, honestly, most plant safety lists are incomplete or confusing. Think of this as your Bengal plant survival guide. I've learned this the hard way, so you won't have to.

Chapter 4
Plant Safety & Your Botanical Detective

Flowers, Plants, and Your Bengal's Botanical Adventures

Imagine this: Edan's ears flick as she stalks a sunbeam across your kitchen, then veers, eyes wide and hungry, toward your beloved Monstera. Stormy, always the connoisseur, hops onto a shelf to pass judgment. In this home, every leafy green is up for inspection (and sometimes, a suspicious nibble).

Why Are Bengals So Obsessed with Plants?

These cats aren't merely curious; they're like detectives with tails! Movement, unfamiliar scents, and that intriguing rustling turn your living room into a jungle for a Bengal. Each plant presents a puzzle, and often, the solution is to chew on it.

The Not-So-Funny Side: Toxic Plants to Avoid

Bengal curiosity can be dangerous. Some plants pose serious risks. Even a small bite could lead to vomiting, drooling, or worse. Always keep a list of toxic plants nearby and have a basic pet first aid kit ready. Toxic Plant List:

- Lilies (all types, including peace lily, daylily, tiger lily, Easter lily)
- Tulips
- Daffodils
- Hyacinth
- Cyclamen
- Kalanchoe

- Aloe vera
- Sago palm
- Oleander
- Dieffenbachia (dumb cane)
- English ivy
- Snake plant
- Jade plant
- Poinsettia
- Bird of paradise
- Dracaena
- Philodendron
- Chrysanthemum

If you suspect your Bengal is up to leafy mischief, contact your vet. Bring a plant sample if possible, every minute counts in your home jungle.

CHAPTER 4
PLANT SAFETY & YOUR BOTANICAL DETECTIVE

Toxic Temptations: What Not to Let Your Bengal Taste

Not all greens are good. Here's your go-to Bengal plant safety table:

Bengal Plant Safety table

Plant Name	Common Symptoms	Emergency Action
Lilies (Lilium/Daylily)	Vomiting, lethargy, kidney failure	Call vet immediately, bring plant sample.
Sago Palm	Vomiting, seizures, liver failure	Emergency vet care ASAP, bring sample.
Daffodil	Drooling, vomiting, abdominal pain	Call vet, bring plant sample.
Aloe Vera	Vomiting, diarrhea, lethargy	Call vet, supportive care.
Cyclamen	Drooling, vomiting, seizures	Call vet immediately.
Poinsettia	Mouth/stomach irritation, vomiting	Monitor, call vet if worsens.
Tulip	Drooling, vomiting, skin irritation	Call vet, supportive care.
Peace Lily	Drooling, difficulty swallowing	Call vet immediately.

A Meadow of Curiosity: What Flowers Are Safe for Bengals?

Bengals like Metanoia Frog below have an Olympic-level sense of exploration and relentless curiosity. Daisies (Bellis perennis), as seen covering this garden, are generally safe for cats and non-toxic. However, not all garden visitors are harmless, and even the safest flower can upset a cat's stomach if overindulged.

- **Safe Blooms:** Daisies, marigolds, roses, sunflowers, and cat grass rank among the friendliest flora for feline friends.

- **Cautionary Blooms:** *"Lilies", "tulips",* and *"daffodils"* rank high on the *"watch out!"* list, as they are toxic to cats.
- **Why Supervision Matters:** Even the investigation of non-toxic plants can cause mild stomach upsets if munched in excess or if pesticides have been used.

Bengal-Proofing Your Indoor Jungle

- Hang risky plants up high, use closed doors, and pick sturdy shelves.
- Offer safe alternatives: cat grass, catnip, Boston or maidenhair fern, and certain palms (like bamboo palm). *Caution: Spider plants are safe but might trigger Bengal zoomies (energetic, rapid running around!).*
- Keep a toxic plant list on the fridge or with your first aid kit.

CHAPTER 4
PLANT SAFETY & YOUR BOTANICAL DETECTIVE

Tech-Savvy Bengal Safety: Apps to Identify Toxic Plants

There are apps that allow you to take a photo of any plant, whether indoors or outdoors, and instantly tell you if it's toxic to cats.

Recommended apps include:

- Picture This.
- ToxiPets.
- Pet Protect Plan: Toxic Plant.
- Leaf Snap.
- ASPCA Animal Poison Control Center (APCC).

No app is flawless; if you're ever unsure, keep the plant out of reach and consult your vet or poison control center for advice.

"I use PictureThis every time I see a new plant on our walks or in the garden. It has saved me from more than one Bengal-induced panic!"

The Good Green List: Bengal-Approved Plants

Not everything green is forbidden! Edan and Stormy recommend their favorite safe picks:

- **Wheatgrass:** A fiber-filled Bengal snack bar.
- **Catnip:** Tasty and excellent for supervised play.
- **Lemon Balm:** Cat-safe and smells amazing.

- **Spider Plant:** Non-toxic, but may cause minor zoomies.
- **Areca/Bamboo Palm:** Tall, frondy, and completely Bengal chic.
- **Boston Fern:** Excellent Bengal napping zone.
- **Calathea:** Pretty on your shelf, safe for feline explorers.
- **Rattlesnake Plant:** Striking, stylish, and certified safe.

Always verify any new plant with the ASPCA or Pet Poison Helpline before bringing it home; Bengals are excellent product testers.

Bonus Goodie: Printable Bengal Plant-Safety Cheat Sheet

Access the quick-reference PDF, designed for kitchen drawers, pinned to notice boards, or in the cat sitter's hands, in your free resource collection (see page 2).

Bengal Trouble Signs: What to Watch For

Here's your "don't panic, but do act" checklist:

- Unusual drooling/pawing at the mouth.
- Vomiting, diarrhoea, or sudden lethargy.
- Wobbling, seizures, or hiding out of sight.
- Refusing favorite foods.
- Odd vocalizations.

CHAPTER 4
PLANT SAFETY & YOUR BOTANICAL DETECTIVE

Action Plan: Confine your kitty, remove any plant bits, call your vet (bring a sample or photo), and stay calm. Most mild exposures are very treatable with swift care!

- **UK Poison Line:** 01202 509000
- **US ASPCA:** (888) 426-4435
- **Australia:** 1300 869 738

Edan & Stormy Rate the Plants

Plant	Edan's Score	Stormy's Score	Notes
Catnip	🌿🌿🌿🌿	😬🌿🌿	"Not worth the drama." – Stormy
Spider Plant	🌀🌀🌀🌀	🐾🐾	"Zoom party!" – Edan
Boston Fern	😴😴😴	😴😴😴	"Best napping zone."
Peace Lily	😱	🚨	"NO ENTRY!"
Bamboo Palm	🌴🌴🌴🌴	🌿🌿🌿🌿	"Jungle-core aesthetic: approved."

"Confused by a paw print or three? Check for our not-so-scientific but VERY Bengal opinions."

How to Read Our Plant Scores

🌿 = "Yum, give me more!" (Catnip/cat-approved).

😬 = "Bored to whiskers."

🌀 = "Zoomies, inbound!"

🐾 = "Fun for the paws."

😴 = "Ideal for napping; don't wake me."

😎 = "Cool factor: certified."

😱 / 🚨 = "Danger! Strictly forbidden. Tell your humans!"

🌴 = "True jungle vibes."

Chapter 4
Plant Safety & Your Botanical Detective

Activities & Tips

- **Scavenger Hunt:** Walk around your house; check your plants using the list.
- **DIY Cat Café:** Grow cat-safe greens for supervised Bengal munching.
- **Fridge Magnet Alert:** Print the plants table for quick emergency reference.

Edan's Perspective

"I took one bite… Now every visitor hears about it! I'm sticking to cat grass, with a little catnip on Fridays."

Note: This information is based on my research and experience, but if you suspect plant poisoning, always contact your vet immediately. I'm a Bengal owner, not a veterinarian, although sometimes I feel like I should have that qualification by now.

Activity: Bengal-Proofing Scavenger Hunt

- Walk through each room and list anything a curious cat could knock over, chew, or climb.
  - Mark each item as "safe," "needs moving," or "needs securing."
  - Set a timer: how quickly can you Bengal-proof your living room?

Metanoia Frog: *the prince in his Butterfly Jacket Harness, patrolling a meadow of daisies, with every spot on his coat shining like a treasure map waiting to be decoded. The royal inspector examines each blade of grass and delicate petal for secrets. But in the garden jungle, which flowers are safe for such a curious explorer?*

"Now that you've created a safe environment for your Bengal to explore, it's time to understand what drives their exploration instincts. Bengal behavior often puzzles new owners, but once you learn to decode their communication and motivations, their actions start making perfect sense

PART II: UNDERSTANIND YOUR BENGAL

Chapter 5
Bengal Behavior Decoded

Understanding Your Living, Breathing Bengal Dictionary

Bengals aren't just vocal; they're conversationalists with opinions about everything from your breakfast choices to your work-from-home productivity. Living with Edan and Stormy has been like getting a crash course in a new language, one where tail positions, ear angles, and vocal inflections all convey specific meanings.

What I've learned through daily observation: Bengal communication is incredibly sophisticated when you take time to really listen and watch. They're not just making noise, they're having conversations.

Decoding Bengal Body Language

The Tail Telegraph System

When Stormy walks through the room with his tail upright and curled at the tip, he's broadcasting confidence and contentment, basically saying, *"Hey, I'm happy you're here."* But when that same tail begins twitching while he gazes out the window, I know he's spotted something interesting and is mentally planning his hunting strategy.

Bengal Tail Translations (From My Daily Observations):

- **Upright with curl:** Happy, confident greeting.
- **Twitching tip:** Focused attention or mild irritation.
- **Bottle brush:** Startled or genuinely scared.
- **Low and swishing:** Hunting mode or serious annoyance.

The Eyes Have It

Edan's slow blinks are legendary in our house. She'll fix you with those crystal green eyes and deliberately close them slowly, what cat behaviorists call *"kitty kisses."* When I blink back slowly, she often purrs and settles in for extended companionship.

What Those Bengal Eyes Are Telling You:

- **Slow blinks:** Trust and affection.
- **Wide, unblinking stare:** Alert or assessing the situation.
- **Half-closed, relaxed:** Content and comfortable.
- **Dilated pupils:** Excited, scared, or in hunting mode.

CHAPTER 5
BENGAL BEHAVIOR DECODED

The Bengal Vocal Symphony

Chirps, Trills, and the Occasional Opera Performance

Bengals talk a lot. Edan has different meows for *"breakfast is late," "pay attention to me,"* and *"I'm conducting important research under the couch."* Stormy's repertoire includes chirping at birds, trilling when he wants me to follow him somewhere, and the occasional 3 AM serenade that I suspect is just him enjoying his own voice.

Bengal Vocal Dictionary (Based on Living with Two Chatty Cats):

- **Short chirp:** "Hello!" or "Notice me, please."
- **Long trill:** *"Follow me!"* (usually toward food bowl or favorite toy).
- **Demanding yowl:** "Service is required immediately."
- **Window chattering:** "I'm practicing my hunting commentary."
- **Soft purr-meow:** "I love you, but also need something."
- **Silent meow:** The ultimate *"please."* (completely irresistible).

Every Bengal develops its own vocal signature. *"Edan's 3 AM opera performances follow a strict schedule: soft warm-up*

81

meows at 2:47 AM, dramatic crescendos by 3:15, and a grand finale that could wake the dead by 3:30. Stormy provides backup vocals that sound suspiciously like applause."

Why Does My Bengal Nip My Bare Heels?

A Tale of Edan's Shadowy Foot Fetish

Bedtime in my house comes with a purr chorus and a Bengal-shaped heat pack. Edan sprawled luxuriously beside me, her motor running, not a care in the world. Morning? She's right there as my personal alarm clock, following me from room to room with utter devotion. But there's a catch: Edan has a secret mission. The literal moment my bare feet hit the floor (or when I leap into bed at night with ankles exposed), a Bengal strike is imminent. And heaven help me if I try Pilates barefoot; the only survivor in this scenario is a good, thick pair of socks. Edan loves bare ankles like Stormy loves sunbeams; it's a thing.

Why Only Bare Heels?

- **Prey Instinct on Parade:** Edan's wild side is alive and well; her bare skin and wiggling toes look just like prey. The movement, the scent, the sheer drama of bare feet or ankles sets off a daily Bengal *"hunt."*
- **Texture and Sensation:** Edan, like many Bengals, is super sensitive to skin texture. Shoes, socks, slippers? Boring. Uncovered ankles? That's a party for the paws!

- **Routine Ritual:** This isn't a call for attention or boredom; it's sensory magic and routine. If she nips, it's not malicious, just an irresistible urge to *"catch"* what looks like prey to her.

Is It Bad? Should I Worry?

For our household, this is classic Bengal logic, not a sign of trouble, just a quirk of Edan's unique personality. If biting ever gets rough or constant, I will check for stress, but most times, it's just her wild roots showing.

Activities and Tips

- **Sock Shield:** Embrace your inner fashionista, socks are your Pilates (and bedtime) superhero cape.
- **Decoy Chase**: Drag an old sock or toy to divert their ninja tendencies. A little pre-bed play burns out the wild before sleep.
- **"Ouch!" Means Pause**: If your Bengal nips, freeze and let them know it's too rough. They'll start to learn that gentle paws win more snuggles.
- **Pawsitive Distraction:** Fill their day with enriching toys, especially anything that lets her pounce, bite, and *"capture"* things that aren't your ankles.

"If you see exposed ankles, so does your Bengal, prepare for liftoff

Edan says, "I adore following you! But let's be honest, bare ankles are just too much fun to resist. Pilates? More like purr-lates!"

If you share your home (and ankles) with a Bengal, every exposed heel is a story waiting to happen. Socks may win the battle, but Edan's wild heart wins the war on boring feet, every time.

CHAPTER 5
BENGAL BEHAVIOR DECODED

The Daily Wellness Inspection

Every morning at 6:47 AM (Bengal-precision timing), Edan performs what I've come to recognize as her daily wellness check.

She'll leap onto my desk where I'm having coffee, position herself directly in front of my face, and hover her nose exactly one inch from mine. Her green eyes lock onto mine with laser focus while she conducts what appears to be a thorough health assessment through careful breathing analysis.

This isn't a request for attention or treats; this is serious business. She'll hold this position for exactly three seconds, sometimes tilting her head slightly as if cross-referencing her findings with previous data. Then, satisfied with whatever information she's gathered, she'll deliver a slow blink of approval and settle in for breakfast.

The same thing happens whenever I pick her up for cuddles, holding her on her back like a baby. The moment she's in position, up comes that little nose for an immediate wellness check. Apparently, being held requires updated health data before she can properly relax into cuddle mode.

It's become so routine that I now hold perfectly still during her inspection, like a patient cooperating with a very furry, comprehensive doctor.

Stormy's version of this behavior is completely different and infinitely more dramatic. It occurs only when I'm in bed, usually around 2 AM, when he decides that my breathing sounds suspicious and needs immediate investigation. He'll sneak up beside my pillow with the stealth of a secret agent, then place his nose directly above mine, close enough that I can feel his whiskers tickling my cheek but never quite touch.

If I'm genuinely asleep, he'll hover there patiently until some subconscious survival instinct wakes me to find two glowing eyes studying my face with the intensity of a medical examiner. The moment I open my eyes and prove I'm alive, he'll purr once, a single note of satisfaction, and curl up beside me like his nocturnal wellness duties are complete.

Both behaviors puzzled me until I realized they were conducting entirely different types of health assessments; each ideally suited to their individual personalities and our specific relationship dynamics.

CHAPTER 5
BENGAL BEHAVIOR DECODED

The Almost-Touch: Understanding Bengal Space Negotiations

When Edan and Stormy approach my face with that intense, almost-touching-but-not-quite nose positioning, they're conducting what I call *"human wellness checks."* What I have learned is that this behavior combines several feline communication methods:

- **Temperature Assessment**: Cats can detect subtle temperature changes through proximity. They're checking if you're running a fever or feeling unwell, a survival instinct from their wild ancestry, where sick group members needed monitoring.
- **Scent Investigation**: Your breath carries information about your health, what you've eaten, and your emotional state. The close approach allows them to gather this data without the commitment of actual nose contact.
- **Greeting Protocol**: In cat society, nose-to-nose touching is an intimate greeting reserved for trusted family members. By approaching but not quite touching, they're offering the greeting while respecting your species differences; they've learned humans don't always appreciate wet nose contact.
- **Attention Assessment**: They're checking if you're truly awake and available for interaction, or just

pretending to be alert. The proximity tests your response level.
- **Affection Display:** This behavior often occurs during their most loving moments; it's their way of saying *"I trust you completely"* without crossing human personal space boundaries they've learned through experience.
- **What It Means:** When both cats do this consistently, it indicates complete trust and acceptance. They've incorporated you into their social structure as a valued family member worthy of intimate greeting protocols, just adapted for your human sensibilities.

Mood Decoder

Every Bengal has a whole spectrum of facial expressions; consider this your secret codebook! From wide-eyed wonder to that classic *"Are you serious?"* stare, your Bengal's face is a billboard for their mood. Reading these cues helps deepen your bond and keeps you one step ahead of their next wild idea!

"How to read a Bengal: four faces, twelve opinions, zero regrets. The mood swings are real, blink and you'll miss one!"

CHAPTER 5
BENGAL BEHAVIOR DECODED

Activity: Bengal Mood Decoder

Watch your Bengal for a day and write down its most dramatic pose or sound. What do you think they meant? Try to *"translate"* their message and see if you can respond in a way that makes them happy.

With eyes like these, Edan could talk me into anything: treats, playtime, or maybe just handing over the whole house!

The Velcro Cat Phenomenon

Bengals earn the nickname *"Velcro cats"* honestly. They don't just tolerate your presence; they want to participate in your daily activities. Edan supervises my morning routine from the bathroom counter, while Stormy feels compelled to inspect and approve every meal I prepare.

"Bathroom visits become supervised activities where your Bengal serves as quality control inspector, bathroom tissue consultant, and moral support coordinator. Stormy rates every bathroom experience on a scale of 1-10 based on optimal water temperature and adequate petting access."

What "Velcro Cat" Actually Means in Daily Life:

- Bathroom visits become supervised activities.
- Work-from-home means feline coworkers.
- Cooking involves quality control specialists.
- Reading requires sharing your lap/book and attention.

Why This Behavior Makes Sense: In my experience, this isn't clinginess; it's Bengal intelligence seeking engagement. They want to understand what you're doing and often figure out how to help (or at least how to make it more interesting).

CHAPTER 5
BENGAL BEHAVIOR DECODED

"One evening, as I was deep in work at my desk, Edan decided my productivity needed a feline intervention."

She leapt onto my desk and placed her toy mouse right on my keyboard, gazing at me expectantly. When I ignored her, she disappeared for a moment, only to return with a second mouse and drop it on the keys, as if to say, *"Now will you play?"*

Edan's idea of productivity: playtime with the mouse, whether I'm ready for it or not!

Zoomies, Water Obsessions, and Other Bengal Specialties

The Midnight Racing Circuit

Bengal zoomies usually happen when they have energy to burn and limited appropriate outlets. In our house, the evening zoomies circuit includes the hallway, living room, and occasionally a dramatic leap onto the cat tree for a grand finale.

When Zoomies Are Normal vs. Concerning:

- **Normal:** Short bursts (5-15 minutes) with obvious triggers like post-litter box relief or pre-meal excitement.
- **Concerning:** Constant restlessness, inability to settle, or zoomies replacing standard sleep patterns.

Activity: Zoomie Tracker

Keep a simple log: What time do your Bengal's zoomies happen? Where do they run?

Do they have a favorite *"track"* or time of day? This helps you plan playtime to match their energy. Share your results with fellow Bengal owners for a laugh.

Chapter 5
Bengal Behavior Decoded

The Great Water Fascination

The Bengals' obsession with water goes beyond quirky mischief; it's part of their DNA. Their wild ancestors, the Asian leopard cats, were stream fishers, so it's no surprise when your Bengal dunks toys, paws at toilets, or leaps into the tub for a splash. In my home, Stormy has tried to *"help"* wash dishes, and Edan once figured out how to nudge the faucet on.

Managing Bengal Water Play (From Experience):

- Use heavy, spill-proof bowls and splash mats.
- Accept that bathroom supervision is part of Bengal territory management.
- Consider supervised splash sessions in bathtubs for water-loving cats.
- Always keep toilet lids down (trust me on this one).

Tip: I let my Bengals play with water in a safe spot to satisfy their curiosity and avoid messes elsewhere.

Edan's convinced the sink is her personal water park; I guess I'll brush my teeth when she's done with her splash session!

CHAPTER 5
BENGAL BEHAVIOR DECODED

When Bengal Behaviors Need Attention

Pica and Non-Food Chewing

Edan once decided that shoelaces were a delicacy worth sampling. This behavior, called pica, can range from harmless exploration to dangerous ingestion of non-food items.

What I've Learned About Managing Pica:

- Stress, boredom, and curiosity are common triggers.
- Provide appropriate chewing alternatives (such as silver vine sticks, dental toys).
- Keep tempting items out of reach.
- If ingestion occurs or behavior becomes obsessive, consult your vet.

This is one area where professional guidance is essential. While some chewing is normal exploration, pica can be dangerous and may require veterinary intervention.

Is it Just for Fun?

Sometimes, yes, Bengals (and other cats) may chew on non-food items simply out of curiosity or because it's entertaining. Their playful, energetic nature means they love to explore the world with their mouths. However, if the chewing becomes frequent or obsessive, it's important to rule out boredom, stress, or medical issues, as true pica can be risky to their health.

Separation Anxiety Signals

When I came home after a weekend trip to find Edan had relocated several items from my dresser to her favorite sleeping spot, I realized she'd been coping with separation stress in her own way. Bengal separation anxiety can be subtle or dramatic.

Signs I've Learned to Recognize:

- Destructive behavior only when you're away
- Excessive vocalization upon return
- Changes in eating or grooming habits
- Relocating owner's belongings (Edan's specialty)

"Why play with toys when you can sample the holiday decor? Bengal kittens: curious, clever, and in desperate need of kitten-proofing. (Pro-tip: Lights are for looking, not for lunch!)"

What Has Worked for Us:

- Gradual departures starting with short absences.
- Interactive toys for solo entertainment.
- Familiar scents (worn t-shirts in sleeping areas).
- Consistent routines that build predictability.

Building Trust Through Understanding

The Great Escape Artists

One afternoon, I found our front door slightly ajar and both cats casually sitting on the porch like they owned the neighborhood. Stormy had learned to operate the door handle while Edan pushed it open. Their teamwork was impressive and slightly terrifying.

What This Taught Me:

- Bengal intelligence requires mental challenges.
- Problem-solving is entertainment for them.
- Underestimating their capabilities leads to surprises.
- Secure latches aren't suggestions, they're necessities.

Bonding Activities That Actually Work

Daily Interactions That Build Trust:

- Interactive play sessions with wand toys.
- Clicker training for mental stimulation.
- Quiet companionship during your daily activities.
- Respecting their boundaries (forcing affection backfires).

The Most Effective Bonding Strategy:

In my experience, the best bonding happens when you become genuinely interested in what interests your Bengal. When Edan brings me her toy mouse for fetch, she's inviting me into her world; accepting that invitation strengthens our relationship.

Activity: Bengal Behavior Journal

Keep a simple log for one week, noting:

- Times when your Bengal is most vocal or active.
- Specific triggers for different behaviors.
- Which bonding activities does your cat enjoy most?
- Any concerning patterns that might need professional attention.

CHAPTER 5
BENGAL BEHAVIOR DECODED

This record becomes invaluable for vet visits, behavioral consultations, or simply understanding your cat's unique patterns.

Edan's Favorite game? Fetching her mouse and dropping it at my feet like a pro retriever.

Edan's Perspective:

"You humans are finally starting to understand. When I chirp at you, it means 'engage with me now,' not 'maybe later when you finish that boring task.' I communicate clearly, slow blinks mean I trust you, bringing toys means playtime, and strategic placement of items means I'm redesigning your space for better functionality."

Stormy's Perspective:

"I believe in clear communication through demonstration. If I sit on your keyboard, it means your computer work is less important than petting me. If I follow you around commenting on everything, I'm being helpful by providing running commentary on your daily activities. Understanding each other makes everything smoother."

Inclusion and Diversity: Every Bengal Deserves a Soft Spot

Edan and Stormy's *"New Friend"* Discovery

On a rainy afternoon, Edan gazed suspiciously at a unique kitten toy, which had three legs and a wild, joyful wobble. Stormy, ever the diplomat, sniffed and then curled protectively around the newcomer. Soon, both Bengals were instructing their new playmate in the art of chasing dust bunnies, demonstrating that love and adventure come in a variety of forms and sizes.

Chapter 5
Bengal Behavior Decoded

Welcoming All Bengals: Special Needs and Diverse Abilities

Bengals, like every cat, are born with unique bodies, quirks, and talents. Some have hearing or vision differences, a missing paw, or simply age into their special needs. A truly inclusive home means celebrating every Bengal's individuality and making small adjustments so every cat can thrive.

Tips for Including Bengals with Disabilities or Special Needs:

- **Mobility Aids:** Use ramps, wide shelves, or low-entry litter boxes for Bengals with joint issues or limb differences.
- **Sensory Adaptations:** Deaf Bengals rely on vibration, stamp softly on the floor to *"call"* them and use visual cues for training. Visually impaired Bengals appreciate consistency in furniture placement and safe, familiar spaces.
- **Safe Zones:** Provide cozy, draft-free beds and clear, accessible pathways to food, water, and favorite perches for seniors or less-mobile cats.
- **Patience and Celebration:** Embrace the quirks; wobbly pounces, slower chases, or quiet cuddles are all wins. These activities are part of your Bengal's unique journey, and you should celebrate every milestone, big or small.

- **Community Connection:** Reach out to online groups or your vet for advice on adaptive enrichment and care; cat lovers worldwide are full of creative ideas.Activities & Tips for Readers
- **Bengal Accessibility Check:** Get down to the cat level and explore your home for tricky corners or high steps. Consider adding a ramp, rearranging furniture, or creating a *"runway"* along the floor to facilitate easy navigation.
- **Special Abilities Journal:** Jot down your Bengal's unique abilities, such as a one-eyed ninja leap or a silent meow, and celebrate what makes your cat special.
- True Bengal spirit is about welcoming adventure and celebrating every difference, big or small. Creating a welcoming environment transforms your home into a haven for every wild heart; after all, the quirkiest Bengals often have the best stories (and the snuggliest naps).

CHAPTER 5
BENGAL BEHAVIOR DECODED

It appears that someone is prepared to tackle those challenging troubleshooting tables, or perhaps even just the mouse! Never forget, Bengal cats don't just bring their energy to playtime; sometimes, they bring it straight to your keyboard. Expect unsolicited 'help' on all technical matters, such as chasing cursors and providing critical commentary on your typing.

Behavior Troubleshooting Table: Quick-Reference for Bengal Owners

A Bengal's bold spirit comes with occasional mischief; sometimes, even the best-prepared owner hits a behavior speed bump. This at-a-glance table brings together the most common Bengal (and general cat) behavior challenges, with clear *"why it happens"* and *"top fix"* guidance to make troubleshooting straightforward, quick, and a bit more light-hearted. Perfect for keeping beside the cat tree or taped to your fridge!

Behavior Problem Quick-Reference Table

Problem	Possible Causes	Top Fixes & Tips
Excessive Meowing/Noisy Nights	Boredom, hunger, attention-seeking, stress	More evening play, puzzle feeders, ignore reward-seeking meows, regular routines
Scratching Furniture/Carpet	Natural instinct, boredom, stress, need to mark	Provide tall scratching posts, use horizontal scratchers, reward use, relocate posts near old targets
Biting/Sudden Aggression	Overstimulated play, fear, frustration, medical	Pause play before overstimulation, redirect to toys, gentle handling, vet check for pain/stress
Inappropriate Urination/Marking	Dirty box, unsuited litter, territory stress, health	Clean box daily, add boxes (1 per cat + 1), stress reduction, vet check urinary issues, spay/neuter advice
Destructive Chewing (Pica)	Boredom, teething (kittens), stress, diet lack	More play, safe chew toys, enrich feeding, check for deficiencies, vet if persistent
Climbing Where Prohibited	Instinct, lack of vertical spaces	Install shelves/cat trees, make forbidden spots less tempting, reward "legal" climbing spots
Over-Grooming/Licking	Anxiety, allergies, pain (medical)	Vet check for allergies/pain, increase enrichment, use calming aids
Fearfulness/Hiding	New home, loud noises, limited socialization	Gradual introductions, create safe zones, patient encouragement, never force interaction
Obsessive Stalking/Hunting Play	Strong prey drive, under-stimulated	Daily energetic play, rotate toys, introduce treat puzzles to redirect energy
Litter Box Avoidance	Box too small/dirty, wrong location/type, stress	Larger/cleaner box, move to quiet spot, try box and litter options, rule out health problems
Aggression With Other Pets	Territory, poor introductions, redirected stress	Slow introductions, pheromone diffusers, separate resources, plenty of perches

Tip: Always rule out medical causes (especially pain, illness, and bladder trouble) before assuming a behavior is "just" naughtiness or Even Edan would agree, a surprise from the vet is scarier than a surprise from Stormy!

Chapter 5
Bengal Behavior Decoded

How to Use This Table

- **Pin it to your fridge** or inside the cover of your behavior chapter for fast reference.
- When a new issue pops up, check the *"Possible Causes";* most Bengal quirks have an underlying need or stressor.
- Try the *"Top Fixes & Tips,"* and if the problem persists, seek advice from your vet or a qualified feline behaviorist.

Bengals are clever, energetic, and sometimes exhausting. Having a quick-troubleshooting table equips new owners with confidence and compassion, reminding you that most feline *"problems"* are just Bengal superpowers ready for redirection. Give each issue a little attention, patience, and a sprinkle of humor, and even the wildest Bengal drama can become just another story to tell.

Activity

- **Behavior Detective Challenge:** For each problem, jot down when and where it happens. Is it before dinner? During a storm? Once a new pet has arrived, proceed. Patterns reveal triggers. Gently test one solution at a time before moving on to the next.

- **Bonding Game:** Track improvements (or creative new behaviors) in a journal with your Bengal's reactions, and reward successes with an extra treat or new toy

"A Bengal's motto: Why use the bowl when you can drink straight from the source? Hydration level, expert. Supervision, strongly recommended!"

Chapter 5
Bengal Behavior Decoded

Edan's Perspective:

"You humans are finally starting to understand. If I chirp at you, it means 'Play,' not 'Wait until you're done with your coffee.' I talk because I have things to say, and if you're not listening, I'll talk louder. Let's see if you can keep up."

Stormy's Perspective:

"Life's not a race, unless Edan's chasing the mouse. I like to take my time, stroll around, and enjoy the view (and maybe block your path for a cuddle). If you hear a crash in the night, it was probably Edan. I was just observing."

Final Thoughts

Understanding Bengal behavior isn't about controlling or changing them; it's about building a communication bridge that works for both species. Every chirp, tail position, and midnight zoomie session is your Bengal sharing information about their needs, feelings, and assessment of the current situation.

What surprised me most was discovering how much the Bengals actually communicate when you learn to listen and observe. They're incredibly expressive cats who want to be understood, not just tolerated.

The key is patience, observation, and genuine curiosity about what makes your individual Bengal tick. Some days you'll feel like a detective solving behavioral mysteries; other days you'll be amazed by how clearly your cat communicates their needs. Both experiences are part of the adventure of sharing your life with these remarkable cats.

Remember: Every Bengal is unique, but they all share that wild intelligence and desire for meaningful interaction. When you meet them on their terms, they'll reward you with a relationship unlike any other pet ownership experience.

"Understanding your Bengal's behavior and communication is essential, but many new owners also wonder about the beautiful variety within the breed itself. While personality matters far more than appearance, knowing about the

CHAPTER 5
BENGAL BEHAVIOR DECODED

different Bengal types can help you appreciate the stunning diversity you might encounter."

Chapter 6
Meet the Bengal Family

Now that you understand what makes Bengals unique, let's explore the beautiful diversity within the breed. When I first started researching Bengals, I was overwhelmed by all the different patterns and colors. *"Silver spotted," "brown marble," "snow lynx,"* it felt like learning a new language. But here's what I wish someone had told me: while the coat patterns are stunning, what matters most is finding a Bengal whose energy level and personality match your lifestyle, not just your aesthetic preferences.

Both Edan and Stormy are brown-spotted Bengals, showcasing the stunning rosettes and marbling that first drew me to the breed. While they share the same base color, their patterns tell very different visual stories, and more importantly, they each have unique personalities that aren't related to their coat patterns.

Understanding Bengal Patterns: The Practical Reality

Think of Bengal patterns like fingerprints; each one is unique, yet they all fit into main categories that can help you identify what you're looking at.

Chapter 6
Meet the Bengal Family

The Basic Pattern Types:

- **Spotted/Rosetted:** The classic *"mini leopard"* look with distinct spots or rosettes.
- **Marbled:** Swirling patterns that create flowing, artistic designs.
- **Combination:** Some Bengals show both patterns (like Stormy's marbling mixed with spots).

What This Actually Means for Daily Life: From my experience living with both pattern types, the visual differences are striking but don't influence personality, care needs, or behavior. Edan's sharp rosettes don't make her more active than Stormy's flowing marble patterns make him calmer. The patterns are beautiful to look at, but personality always matters more.

Living Art: When Your Cat is a Conversation Piece

Edan demonstrates that the Bengals are walking masterpieces. Her coat serves as a canvas of bold rosettes and swirls, outlined in rich, warm tones. Sometimes, when the sunlight streams in just right, her fur glitters as if it were dusted with gold. I still remember the first time a friend visited and gasped, *"She looks like a tiny leopard!"* Edan, of course, took this as her cue to strike a regal pose on the windowsill, basking in admiration as if she were the star of her own gallery opening.

BENGAL CATS YOUR GUIDE FOR FIRST TIME OWNERS

The Reality of Living with "Living Art"

- You'll have more photos of your cat than most family members.
- Strangers will stop to admire and ask about your Bengal.
- Every sunbeam becomes a photo opportunity.
- Your cat will somehow know they're gorgeous and act accordingly.

What I didn't expect: the patterns seem to shift and change as they move and as the lighting varies throughout the day. Edan looks golden in the morning light, rich chocolate by evening.

Bengal Rosettes: Edan not only lights up the room, she also sparkles in it!

CHAPTER 6
MEET THE BENGAL FAMILY

Color Varieties: Beyond Brown and Black

Brown/Black Series: (Like Edan and Stormy)

This is what most people picture when they think *"Bengal,"* warm browns ranging from cool chocolate to rich gold, with black markings that can be solid spots, flowing marble patterns, or a combination of both.

Living with Brown Bengals:

- Show dirt less than lighter colors (a practical consideration for active cats).
- Photographs beautifully in natural light.
- Classic *"leopard"* appearance that everyone recognizes.

Silver Series: The Dramatic Contrast

Silver Bengals create a striking visual with their silver-white coats and bold black markings. The contrast between the cool silver background and dark spots or marbles draws the eye, often accented by vibrant green or gold eyes, which look stunning in photos.

The Silver Reality:

- Show every speck of dust, but somehow still look elegant.
- Create a dramatic visual impact that makes visitors do double-takes.
- Often have piercing green eyes that miss nothing.

Snow Series: The Pale Beauties

Snow Bengals come in three types: Lynx, Mink, and Sepia. Snow Lynx typically have blue eyes, while Snow Mink and Sepia often have aqua to gold eyes. They are born nearly white and develop their markings over time.

The Snow Bengal Reality:

- Markings develop and change during the first few years.
- Eye colors range from striking blue to aqua to gold, depending on the variety.
- Like having a tiny snow leopard in your living room.

Specialty Colors: The Rare and Beautiful

Charcoal, blue, and melanistic Bengals are rarer but equally beautiful, each with its own unique traits and dedicated fans. These specialty types usually cost more and have longer waitlists because of their scarcity.

CHAPTER 6
MEET THE BENGAL FAMILY

The Specialty Bengal Reality:

- Charcoal Bengals sport dramatic *"Zorro masks"* and cape patterns that add mystery to any base color.
- Blue Bengals display cool blue-grey tones instead of traditional browns, creating an ethereal appearance.
- Melanistic Bengals are living shadows with *"ghost"* markings visible in bright light, like pocket panthers.

"I've seen from Bengal shows and online groups that fans love every color and pattern—but it's personality that really counts day to day."

Edan's Dream Parade: A Gallery of Bengal Beauty

Sometimes I wonder what Edan dreams about during her afternoon naps. Does she picture a world filled with every kind of Bengal? Here's how I imagine her dream parade...

Common Bengal Types in Edan's Dream Gallery

Each Bengal type below is featured as a guest star in Edan's dream, celebrating the breed's full spectrum of beauty, personality, and fun. For each one, you'll find a vivid description, what makes them unique, and owner tips.

Each Bengal is a vivid masterpiece, with a coat as unique as its personality. This chapter is more than just an encyclopedia of spots and swirls; it's your invitation to the grand *"Bengal Parade."* Edan's dream gallery is about to come alive, with each Bengal type stepping in for their close-up.

Brown Spotted Bengal - *"The Classic Beauty"*

Edan stretched and blinked, sunlight spilling across her favorite windowsill. The remnants of her wild dream still shimmered in her mind, but as she shook off sleep, Edan realized she was the dream. This time, fully awake, her senses sharp, her paws poised to prowl.

This is the Bengal most people imagine: golden coats with bold rosettes, like Edan and Stormy. Their *"poker dot socks"* and striped markings on their legs look like they're dressed for a jungle fashion show. Those bright green or gold eyes? Each one looks like they have stepped out of a wildlife documentary.

What Makes Them Special:

- Classic leopard appearance that everyone recognizes.
- Markings that seem to dance and shift as they move.
- Perfect balance of wild looks with domestic personality.

CHAPTER 6
MEET THE BENGAL FAMILY

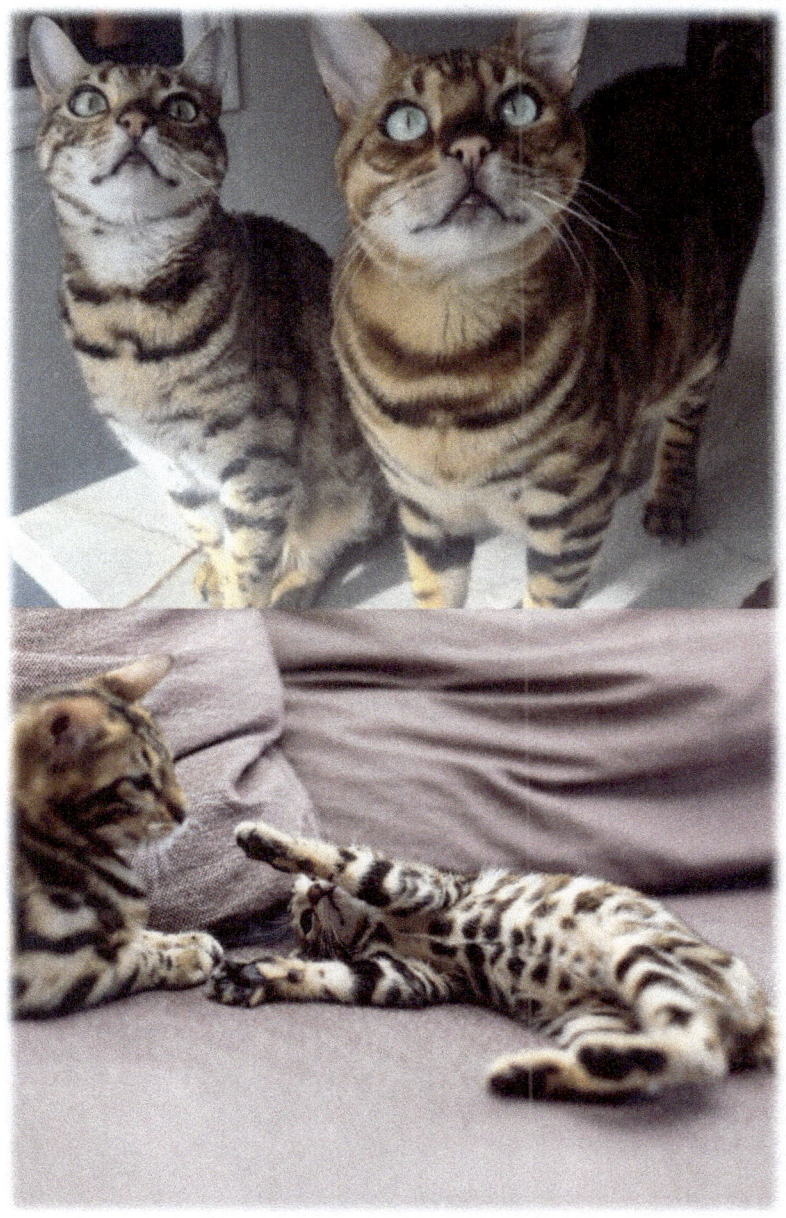

Who needs store-bought socks when you've got poker dots, stripes, and wild style built in!

Silver Spotted Bengal - "The Snowstorm Surprise"

In Edan's dream, a shimmering figure leapt onto the windowsill, her coat sparkling like moonlight on snow. Each inky spot stood out in bold contrast. Edan froze in amazement. Had a tiny snow leopard moved in overnight?

Silver Bengals are living contrasts, with cool silver fur and bold black spots that create striking visual drama. They photograph like professional models but still manage to gather dust bunnies during their behind-the-washing-machine adventures.

The Silver Reality:

- Stunning visual impact in any room.
- Show every speck of dust (but somehow still look elegant).
- Often have piercing green eyes that miss nothing.

CHAPTER 6
MEET THE BENGAL FAMILY

The silver spotted Bengal, Is it a Bengal or a snow leopard in disguise? Either way, she's only hunting for snacks and sunbeams!

Snow Lynx Bengal - "The Frozen Adventure"

Suddenly, a flash of white darted across Edan's dream-snow. A Snow Lynx Bengal bounded through a winter wonderland, its ivory coat blending perfectly with the frosty world, those dazzling blue eyes sparkling like sapphires.

Born almost white with markings that develop over time, these Bengals look like they stepped out of a winter fairy tale. Those striking blue eyes make everyone stop and stare - and the cats know it.

Living with Snow Bengals:

- Markings continue developing for the first 2-3 years.
- Blue eyes that photograph beautifully.
- Light coloring shows dirt quickly but also highlights their elegant movement.

Chapter 6
Meet the Bengal Family

The Snow Lynx Bengal - Is it a snowball, a lynx, or a Bengal in disguise? Edan's dream proving that winter white is always in season, especially when paired with a blue-eyed stare.

Charcoal Bengal - "The Shadow Stalker"

A living shadow moved through Edan's dream, masked and enigmatic. The Charcoal Bengal's rich smoky coat and striking "Zorro mask" caused even Edan to pause in awe.

These are the mysterious ninjas of the Bengal world. Their dark *"cape"* along the back and distinctive facial mask give them an air of intrigue. They move as if they're plotting something - and they probably are!

Living with Charcoal Bengals:

- Show a dramatic contrast that photographs beautifully, but dust is clearly visible on the dark fur.
- Often have intense, piercing eyes that seem to see everything you're doing.
- Their *"mysterious"* appearance matches equally enigmatic personalities; they're the cats who appear silently behind you.

CHAPTER 6
MEET THE BENGAL FAMILY

The Charcoal Bengal - Is it a Bengal or a tiny cat burglar in disguise? Either way, she's only after your snacks (and maybe your hair ties)!

Silver Marbled Bengal - "The Abstract Artist"

A Bengal streaked through Edan's dream, resembling more a Jackson Pollock painting than a leopard. Swirls, streaks, and splashes of silver moved across his fur in fluid, water-like patterns.

Instead of spots, these Bengals wear flowing, marble patterns that look hand-painted. Each one is a unique masterpiece; no two marbled Bengals ever look the same.

Living with Silver Marbled Bengals:

- Absolutely stunning visual impact, making them living art pieces in your home.
- Every movement shows off their flowing patterns in different ways as light catches the marble.
- Their unique markings ensure you'll never mistake your cat for another; each pattern is completely individual.

Chapter 6
Meet the Bengal Family

The Silver Marbled Bengal. Is it a Bengal or a walking work of art? Either way, she's only signing autographs for treats!

Melanistic Bengal - "The Panther in the Parlor"

On a stormy dream-night, Edan spotted a shadowy figure with a coat as dark as velvet and eyes gleaming like lanterns. The Melanistic Bengal moved with silent confidence, every bit the pocket panther.

These rare beauties are cloaked in deep black or chocolate brown, sometimes with *"ghost"* spots visible only in bright sunlight. They're the most mysterious of all Bengals, moving like tiny panthers through your living room.

Living with Melanistic Bengals:

- Their *"ghost"* spots create an ever-changing appearance depending on the lighting.
- Incredibly striking presence that makes visitors do double-takes; they really do look like miniature panthers.
- Often have golden or green eyes, which create a dramatic contrast against their dark coats.

CHAPTER 6
LY

The Melanistic Bengal, is it a Bengal or a pocket-sized panther? She is hunting for the warmest lap in the house.

What This Means for Choosing Your Bengal

The Most Important Lesson I've Learned: When choosing your Bengal, remember that all these beautiful varieties share the same wonderful Bengal personality. Whether your future companion ends up being a classic brown beauty like Edan, a striking silver stunner, or something completely unexpected, what matters most is the bond you'll build together.

Focus on These Factors Instead:

- Energy level that matches your lifestyle.
- Socialization and temperament.
- Health history and breeder reputation.
- Your connection with the individual cat.

Patterns don't predict personality. A marble Bengal isn't necessarily calmer than a spotted one, and silver Bengals aren't more dramatic than browns (though Edan might disagree with that last point).

CHAPTER 6
MEET THE BENGAL FAMILY

Edan dreams of being a leopard one day... Stormy's just here for the nap credits. Observe your Bengals' sleeping habits, you might just discover your own cat's secret ambition during a catnap!

CHAPTER 6
MEET THE BENGAL FAMILY

Bengal Parade: Are All Types Here?

If your Bengal isn't in our parade, don't worry; they're probably just waiting for their debut!

Understanding Bengal Patterns

Bengal cats are renowned for their stunning coat patterns, often envied by cat lovers! Their unique markings blend wild beauty with domestic charm, making each Bengal look like a tiny jungle cat in your living room.

How to Read This Bengal Pattern Illustration

This chart lets you explore Bengal cat patterns and colors at a glance! Here's how to decode what you're seeing:

Columns show the color variation moving from left to right:

1. Brown/Orange.
2. Silver.
3. Snow (Lynx or Cream).
4. Charcoal.
5. Melanistic (Black).

Rows display the three main Bengal patterns for each color:

- **Top row:** Spotted/rosetted patterns, classic *"wildcat"* look.
- **Middle row:** Middle row: Marbled patterns, swirling, horizontal designs unique to Bengal.
- **Bottom row:** "Clouded" or heavier marble/rosette variation, larger markings with bold, high-contrast shapes.

To use this chart, select a color column and observe how all three Bengal patterns (spotted, marbled, and clouded/heavily marked) appear within that color. You'll quickly see that Bengals can be both consistent and endlessly unique!

Understanding these patterns will help you distinguish a marbled masterpiece from a classic spotted Bengal the next time you join the Bengal Parade.

CHAPTER 6
MEET THE BENGAL FAMILY

"A Bengal to match every mood: from wild leopard to swirling marbles, and every color under the (cat) sun. Try not to pick a favorite, it's impossible."

Understanding Your Bengal's Unique Story

Every Bengal's coat tells a story of genetics, development, and individual uniqueness. Edan's bold rosettes reflect confidence and drama. At the same time, Stormy's flowing marble patterns seem to match his laid-back, artistic approach to life, but these connections are probably more about my imagination than scientific fact.

What Actually Matters:

- How your Bengal interacts with you and your family.
- Their individual personality quirks and preferences.
- Whether their energy level works with your lifestyle.
- The daily joy they bring to your home.

Activity: Bengal Pattern Appreciation

Take photos of your Bengal in various lighting conditions throughout the day. Observe how their patterns appear to change and shift. Record their unique markings; they truly are one of a kind.

Edan's Perspective:

"Obviously, I'm the perfect example of Bengal beauty, with classic rosettes, a dramatic presence, and natural modeling instincts." But I suppose all Bengal patterns have their charm. *"The key is finding humans who appreciate feline artistry and understand that we're not just pets, we're living masterpieces who deserve appropriate admiration."*

Stormy's Perspective:

"Every Bengal is beautiful in its own way. Some have bold spots, others have flowing marble patterns, some are silver, and others are gold. What matters most is finding humans who see past the pretty coat to the personality underneath. Though I admit, having gorgeous markings doesn't hurt when it comes to getting extra treats and attention."

CHAPTER 6
MEET THE BENGAL FAMILY

Final Thoughts

The Bengal *"family"* includes a stunning variety of colors and patterns, each more beautiful than the last. But after living with Edan and Stormy, I've come to see that the true beauty of Bengals isn't in their coats but in their personalities, intelligence, and the special bond they form with their humans.

Whether your Bengal ends up being a classic spotted beauty, an artistic marbled stunner, or a rare color variety, what matters most is the daily adventure you share together. The patterns are just the beautiful wrapping paper around the real gift, a cat who will challenge you, entertain you, and love you with wild-hearted devotion.

When choosing your Bengal, follow your heart to find a personality that matches yours. The stunning coat is assured; the bond you build is what you'll cherish for years.

"Whether your Bengal turns out to be a classic spotted beauty or a striking marbled stunner, they all have the same nutritional needs. Now that you recognize the variety within the breed, let's focus on one of the most important parts of daily care: feeding your Bengal properly."

Interactive Quiz: Which Bengal Are You?

Edan's Personality Parade

It was a lazy Sunday afternoon when Edan stretched out on the windowsill, watching the clouds drift by. Stormy, ever the mischief-maker, pounced onto the sofa and declared, *"If I were a different Bengal, I'd be a snow leopard today!"*

Edan rolled her eyes. *"You? Please. I'm the Queen of the Quiz. Let's see what kind of Bengal you really are!"* And so, the great Bengal personality quiz was born.

Which Bengal Type Matches Your Personality?

Are you a bold explorer, a dreamy sunbeam chaser, or a mysterious midnight prowler? Answer the questions below and tally your results to discover your inner Bengal!

CHAPTER 6
MEET THE BENGAL FAMILY

Question 1: How do you spend a lazy Sunday?

Option	Description
A	Climbing every shelf and plotting new adventures.
B	Shimmering in sunbeams like moonlight on snow.
C	Pouncing through a frosty window, dreaming of a winter wonderland.
D	Sneaking through shadows, plotting mysterious adventures.
E	Creating flowing, artistic patterns with my movements.
F	Hiding in the darkest nook, eyes glowing like golden lanterns.

Question 2: What's your dream coat?

Option	Description
A	Golden coat with bold, wild rosettes and "poker dot socks."
B	Silver-white fur that shimmers like moonlight with dramatic black spots.
C	Ivory coat with dazzling blue eyes and markings that develop over time.
D	Deep smoky coat with a dramatic "Zorro mask" and mysterious cape.
E	Flowing marble patterns that look hand-painted in silver and black.
F	Deep black velvet with "ghost" spots visible only in bright light.

CHAPTER 6
MEET THE BENGAL FAMILY

Question 3: What's your favorite toy?

Option	Description
A	Anything that flies, dangles, or can be chased—classic leopard hunting.
B	A shiny ball that glitters and creates dramatic contrasts.
C	A plush snowflake or winter-themed feather wand.
D	A tunnel or dark hiding spot for stealth operations.
E	Flowing ribbon toys that move like abstract art.
F	A laser pointer in a dark room—perfect for shadow stalking.

Question 4: How do you greet strangers?

Option	Description
A	Strut up confidently and demand attention—classic leopard confidence.
B	Observe from a distance, then make a dramatic, shimmering entrance.
C	Watch from the window with those striking blue eyes, then approach.
D	Watch quietly from the shadows, then appear when least expected.
E	Move gracefully like a flowing work of art, mesmerizing everyone.
F	Appear silently like a shadow, then vanish just as mysteriously.

CHAPTER 6
MEET THE BENGAL FAMILY

Question 5: What's your superpower?

Option	Description
A	Classic leopard presence—everyone recognizes my wild beauty immediately.
B	Creating stunning visual drama that makes visitors do double-takes.
C	My blue eyes photograph beautifully, and I look like a winter fairy tale.
D	Moving like I'm plotting something mysterious (and I probably am!).
E	Being a living art piece where every movement shows off flowing patterns.
F	Disappearing and reappearing like a miniature panther.

BENGAL CATS YOUR GUIDE FOR FIRST TIME OWNERS

Quiz Results: Which Bengal Are You?

Count how many times you chose each letter. Your highest total reveals your Bengal type!

Bengal Type	Personality Description
Mostly A's: Brown Spotted Bengal **"The Classic Beauty"**	You're the Bengal everyone pictures first! Like Edan, you have classic leopard presence with bold confidence and natural modeling instincts. Your golden personality and wild rosettes make you the perfect balance of domestic charm and untamed spirit.
Mostly B's: Silver Spotted Bengal **"The Snowstorm Surprise"**	You're a living contrast who creates stunning visual drama wherever you go. Like moonlight on snow, you have that shimmering presence that makes visitors do double-takes. You photograph like a professional model but still collect dust bunnies during adventures.
Mostly C's: Snow Lynx Bengal **"The Frozen Adventure"**	You're the winter fairy tale come to life! With those striking blue eyes that photograph beautifully, you look like you stepped out of a snowy wonderland. Your markings continue developing and changing, just like your personality—always evolving, always captivating.

Chapter 6
Meet the Bengal Family

Bengal Type	Personality Description
Mostly D's: Charcoal Bengal **"The Shadow Stalker"**	You're the mysterious ninja of the Bengal world! That dramatic "Zorro mask" personality matches your enigmatic nature. You move like you're plotting something interesting (and you probably are!), appearing silently with intense, piercing insight.
Mainly E's: Silver Marbled Bengal **"The Abstract Artist"**	You're a walking work of art! Like a Jackson Pollock painting come to life, your flowing patterns and graceful movements mesmerize everyone around you. Each interaction shows off different aspects of your unique personality.
Mainly F's: Melanistic Bengal **"The Panther in the Parlor"**	You're the ultimate shadow expert with pocket-panther presence! Your mysterious, almost magical nature creates an ever-changing appearance depending on the situation. You move through life like a beautiful, confident shadow with golden eyes.

Activities & Tips for Readers

Activity	Description
Share your result	Are you a bold Brown Bengal or a mysterious Melanistic? Tell your family or friends and compare answers!
Photo Challenge	Take a photo of your Bengal (or yourself) that matches your quiz result.
Creative Writing Prompt	Write a short story about your Bengal's secret life as their quiz "type."

CHAPTER 6
MEET THE BENGAL FAMILY

Edan's Perspective:

"I mostly got A's, obviously. But I'll let you join my jungle, no matter your Bengal style. Just don't forget the treats!"

Stormy's Perspective:

"I'm still a classic brown Bengal, but I wouldn't mind dreaming of being a silver marbled masterpiece for a day. More options, more fun!"

Final Thoughts

This quiz celebrates the diverse personalities of Bengals. Whether you're a classic explorer, a shimmering showstopper, or a mysterious shadow stalker, each Bengal (and owner) brings something special to the parade. Enjoy discovering your inner Bengal, and remember, the best answer is always the one that makes you purr!

PART III: DAILY LIFE & CARE

Chapter 7
Feeding Your Bengal

I'll never forget the first time Edan tried raw beef. She pulled a piece off her plate and onto the floor, then made a little *"num num num"* noise, like a song of pure enjoyment. That joyful food song became her signature, and she still does it years later when her meal hits the perfect spot.

What that experience taught me: Bengals often have strong food preferences and aren't afraid to share their opinions. Feeding them well becomes a key part of building your relationship.

Vet's Caution:

Veterinary authorities in Australia, the US, and worldwide generally advise against feeding raw diets to household cats, including Bengals. The main reasons include the risk of dangerous bacteria or parasites and the real danger of nutritional imbalance, especially if raw meals aren't prepared or handled by veterinary professionals. High-quality commercial cat foods are well researched, nutritionally complete, and much safer for most pet owners.

Understanding Bengal Nutrition

Bengals are energetic athletes with big appetites and sensitive stomachs. Their wild ancestry means they thrive on a high-protein, meat-based diet. The right food fuels their zoomies, keeps their coats shiny, and supports their active lifestyles. When choosing a diet, it's essential to balance their wild energy with modern safety. Commercial, research-backed foods (like Royal Canin, Hills, Eukanuba) are tailor-made for Bengals' needs, high-protein, breed-specific, and fortified for long-term health.

- **The Reality Check:** Finding the right food often involves trial, error, and sometimes dramatic reviews of your choices. Edan once staged a hunger strike over a new kibble brand, while Stormy will eat almost anything as long as it's served with proper ceremony.

Raw Diet: The Closest to Nature

Safety Warning – Read Me First:

Raw food diets, while appealing to some owners, carry well-documented risks. If mishandled, they may expose your Bengal and household to Salmonella, Listeria, or other pathogens. Additionally, getting the nutrition right is extremely difficult, especially for essential nutrients like taurine, which cats cannot produce on their own. A taurine deficiency can lead to blindness, heart problems, and more.

CHAPTER 7
FEEDING YOUR BENGAL

Unless guided by a vet or feline nutritionist, feeding raw is not recommended for most pet owners.

- Raw feeding can be advantageous when appropriately done, but it requires research, preparation, and strict adherence to food safety.
- My Experience with Raw: Both Edan and Stormy thrive on raw food, but the preparation time and safety requirements mean it's not our only feeding method. I learned everything from Lyn Dowd at Metanoia Bengals, whose safety guidelines have kept us worry-free.

Lyn Dowd's Essential Safety Rules:

- Freeze chicken for at least 7 days before feeding (reduces parasite risk).
- Freeze red meat for at least 3 days.
- Never give cooked bones (they splinter).
- Portion before freezing for convenience.
- Always thaw in the refrigerator, never on counters.

This advice is from an experienced breeder but always consult your veterinarian about raw feeding. Every cat's needs are different. If you still want to try raw feeding, talk to your vet and get your recipes checked for complete nutrients, especially taurine, calcium, and other essentials. High-quality commercial foods provide balanced nutrition and meet strict safety standards.

Wet Food: The Hydration Hero

Most Bengals enjoy wet food, as it offers great hydration benefits for their kidney health. The wide range of flavors keeps meals engaging, even though storing it may be less convenient than dry food.

Dry Food: The Convenient Backup

High-quality, grain-free dry food is ideal for busy schedules and puzzle feeders. Select options with real meat as the main ingredient and a few fillers.

Mixed Feeding: The Practical Approach

The Feeding Schedule Negotiation

Establishing our current mixed-feeding routine required diplomatic negotiations similar to international relations. Edan preferred her wet food as the main event in the morning, with dry kibble for midday snacking. Stormy wanted damp food for dinner, with puzzle feeders offering entertainment during his afternoon energy peaks.

After weeks of trial and error, we finally settled on a system that suits both personalities: wet food for breakfast, raw food for dinner for both cats (served differently), puzzle feeders rotating during solo play, and high-quality dry food for snacks. This mixed approach provides nutritional variety while keeping both cats happy with their personalized service.

CHAPTER 7
FEEDING YOUR BENGAL

What works in our house might not work in yours. Every Bengal has individual preferences, and finding the right combination often requires experimentation.

Edan's Food Ritual:

Edan insists on dining with the company, often dragging her food next to me. She's an *"affection eater,"* proof that Bengals value mealtime bonding as much as nutrition.

Edan insists dinner tastes better with company; why eat alone when you can bring the feast to your favorite human?

Portion Control: Learning from Experience

The Great Portion Miscalculation Incident

During Edan's first month with us, I carefully followed the feeding guidelines on her kitten food. The package recommended portions for *"active indoor cats,"* and I assumed that included a Bengal. What I hadn't thought about was Edan's own idea of *"active."* While other cats might play for twenty minutes and then nap for three hours, Edan considered every moment awake as athletic training.

Within two weeks, I noticed she was constantly hungry, meowing plaintively at her empty bowl and giving me reproachful looks that clearly communicated my inadequacy as a food provider. When our vet confirmed she was actually underweight despite what seemed like adequate portions, I realized I'd been feeding a feline athlete like a couch potato.

Doubling her portions (under veterinary guidance) transformed her from a constantly hungry kitten into a satisfied, lively Bengal who could focus on key activities like curtain climbing and sock theft instead of always looking for food. This made me realize that Bengal portion guidelines need serious adjustment based on their energy levels.

CHAPTER 7
FEEDING YOUR BENGAL

The "How Much is Enough?" Question

What I learned through trial and error:

- Kittens require frequent, calorie-dense meals (follow your veterinarian's guidance as they grow).
- Adult Bengals typically need 270-360 calories daily, divided into several meals.
  Senior cats usually need fewer calories but higher-quality protein.
  Active Bengals need more food; sedentary Bengals need portion control.

Practical Feeding Guidelines That Work:

- Split daily portions into 2-3 meals.
- Use measuring cups or scales for accuracy.
- Monitor body condition, you should feel but not see ribs.
- Adjust based on activity level, season, and life stage.

Bengal Age / Weight	Meals per Day	Amount per Day	Activity / Notes
Kitten 3–6mo (1–2kg)	3–4	60–120g (10% body wt)	Up portions for growth, split meals for energy
Kitten 6–12mo (2–3kg)	3	90–130g	Add more if growing fast or extremely active
Adult (3–5kg)	2–3	140–250g (3–5% bw)	+10–20% for high-zoomies, reduce for indoor-only
Senior (4–5kg, low act)	2	110–180g	Seniors generally need 10–15% less; monitor for loss

These are general guidelines based on my experience. Your vet can provide specific recommendations for your Bengal's individual needs.

At-a-Glance Bengal Feeding Table

Raw Feeding: The Complete Reality

Building a Balanced Raw Diet

Raw feeding isn't just about throwing meat into a bowl. True nutritional balance requires protein, calcium, organ meats, and essential vitamins.

The Basic Formula That Works:

- 80% muscle meat (chicken, beef, lamb, etc.)
- 10% bone or calcium supplement (eggshell powder works well).
- 10% organ meat (liver, kidney, heart).
- Added vitamins and minerals as needed.

CHAPTER 7
FEEDING YOUR BENGAL

Lyn Dowd's Practical Tips:

- Eggshell powder: Dehydrate, blend to powder, add a pinch for calcium.
- Dehydrated organs: Crumble and rehydrate as needed.
- Seaweed sprinkles: Provides trace minerals.
- Always add water or broth to every meal for hydration.

This information is based on my breeder's experience, but raw feeding can be complicated. Consider consulting a feline nutritionist for tailored advice.

Essential Raw Diet Formula

Ingredient	Amount (per 100g)	Why It's Important
Muscle meat	80g	Protein, energy, amino acids
Edible bone/eggshell	7–10g	Calcium, phosphorus, minerals
Organ meats	5–10g	Vitamins A, D, E, K, taurine
Seaweed (kelp)	Pinch	Iodine, trace minerals
Divetilac powder	Sprinkle	Extra vitamins, minerals
Water/broth	Add as needed	Hydration, kidney support

Taurine – The Critical Bengal Nutrient

Cats, including Bengals, need taurine in their diet to stay healthy. Taurine deficiencies are common in homemade raw diets unless organ meats, especially heart, are included and accurately measured. Commercial foods from reputable brands always add taurine, which helps keep their eyes, hearts, and digestion healthy. Never skip this; always check labels or consult a professional.

Tricks & Tips from Lyn Dowd

- **Eggshell powder:** Dehydrate, blend to powder, add a pinch for easy calcium.
- **Dehydrated organs:** Crumble in, rehydrate as needed.
- **Seaweed sprinkles:** For trace minerals, *little* goes a long way.
- **Divetilac powder:** Try as a warm drink or topper for a vitamin boost.
- **Always hydrate:** Add water or broth to every meal.

Sample Mixed (Raw / Wet / Dry) Feeding Routine

- **Morning:** Wet food (e.g., chicken or turkey).
- **Midday:** High-protein dry kibble (in a puzzle feeder).
- **Evening:** Wet food or a raw treat.
- **Kittens:** Require more frequent, calorie-dense meals; follow breeder or vet guidelines and adjust as they grow.

I adjust portions based on activity, metabolism, and health, and I always provide fresh water.

CHAPTER 7
FEEDING YOUR BENGAL

Chef Edan says, "Meal prep? No problem, I'll paw through the options myself. Don't forget the eggshells; bones are for leaping, not just eating!"

157

The Great Food Preference Discovery

When Stormy became part of our household, I thought he'd like the same food as Edan. However, this lasted only for one meal. Edan eagerly enjoyed her high-quality wet food, while Stormy sniffed it carefully, took a single courteous bite, and then walked away, rejecting it diplomatically, much like a seasoned diplomat negotiating treaties.

After three days of Stormy eating just enough to be polite while clearly hoping for better options, I realized these two needed individualized dining experiences. Edan preferred her wet food at room temperature with a side of kibble for texture variety. Stormy preferred his wet food to be slightly warmed and served without the ceremony that Edan demanded.

This taught me that even within the same household, Bengal food preferences can vary greatly, demanding flexible feeding strategies instead of one-size-fits-all solutions.

Types of Food: Navigating the Options

Walking down the pet food aisle can be overwhelming when you're trying to understand what *"premium," "grain-free,"* and *"breed-specific"* actually mean for your Bengal. After years of reading labels and taste-testing Bengal foods, I've learned that marketing claims matter less than understanding which features truly benefit active, intelligent cats.

CHAPTER 7
FEEDING YOUR BENGAL

What I Look for When Reading Labels:

- **High Meat Content:** The primary ingredient should be a specific meat source (such as chicken, salmon, or lamb) instead of generic *"meat meal"* or grain fillers. Bengals are carnivores with high protein requirements, so meat should be the main component in the ingredient list.

- **Grain-Free Options:** Although not necessary for every cat, many Bengal owners discover that grain-free formulas are effective for cats with sensitive digestion. The energy mainly comes from protein instead of carbohydrate fillers.

- **Breed-Specific Formulations:** Some manufacturers develop Bengal-specific foods formulated for higher energy requirements and larger cat sizes. These typically include increased protein content and kibble sizes suitable for Bengal mouths.

- **Quality Control Standards:** Look for foods made in facilities with strong safety records and transparent sourcing information. Your Bengal's health relies on consistent quality.

- **What the Table Shows:** The accompanying chart shows brands that other Bengal owners often choose, ranging from premium wet foods like Ziwi Peak and Feline Natural, Eukanuba, and Hills Science to breed-specific options like Royal Canin Bengal. These serve as starting points for your own research rather than universal recommendations.

- **The Reality Check:** Even the highest-quality food won't work if your Bengal doesn't like it. I've seen Bengals reject expensive premium foods while happily eating mid-range options that match their specific tastes. Quality matters, but so does individual preference.
- **My Approach:** Start with foods that meet basic quality standards (high meat content, proper protein levels, good manufacturing practices), then observe your Bengal's response to guide your choices. A food that is enthusiastically eaten and provides good energy and healthy coats is better than premium food that remains untouched in the bowl.

Remember: Your veterinarian can offer specific advice based on your Bengal's age, health, and individual needs. Use these options to start discussions rather than as final decisions.

Popular Food Brands for

Brand	Type	Notes
Royal Canin Bengal	Dry	Breed-specific, balanced nutrition
Applaws	Wet/Dry	High meat, grain-free
Ziwi Peak	Air-dried/raw	High-protein, limited ingredients
Black Hawk	Dry	Australian, natural ingredients
Feline Natural	Freeze-dried	Raw, high-protein, easy to store

Chapter 7
Feeding Your Bengal

"There's no one-size-fits-all 'best' food for every Bengal, but these brands are commonly chosen by Bengal owners. Use this as a starting point and consult your vet for personalized advice."

Tips for New Owners

- **Follow package guidelines:** Begin with the recommended amount of your selected food and modify it based on your Bengal's body condition and appetite.
- **Weigh food for accuracy:** Use a kitchen scale for raw or wet food; measure kibble with a constant scoop.
- **Monitor body condition:** You should be able to feel, but not see, your Bengal's ribs. Adjust portions if your cat appears too thin or is starting to get a bit "chunky."
- **Split meals:** Eating several smaller meals mimics natural hunting and helps prevent digestive upset.
- **Consult your vet:** For personalized advice, especially if your Bengal has health problems or is a selective eater.

Food Storage and Safety

The Practical Systems That Work

Raw Food Storage (From Experience):

- Portion into 2 3-day servings before freezing.
- Label everything with contents and the date.
- Thaw only what you need for immediate feeding.
- Keep frozen: Ground meat (3-4 months), whole pieces (6-12 months).

Kitchen Safety Rules:

- Separate cutting boards for raw cat food.
- Clean and sanitize all surfaces promptly.
- Wash your hands thoroughly after handling.
- Store thawed portions in the refrigerator; use within 24 hours.

Reminder: When unsure, focus on safety and proper nutrition. Commercial cat foods from top brands are crafted to support Bengals' active lifestyles and overall health.

The Feeding Ritual: More Than Just Nutrition

Edan's *"Affection Eating"* Phenomenon

Edan doesn't just eat, she performs. She enjoys bringing her food over to wherever I am, curling up beside me at the kitchen counter or on the couch. For her, meals are social occasions, not solitary moments.

CHAPTER 7
FEEDING YOUR BENGAL

What This Taught Me:

- Bengals often prefer eating near their favorite humans.
- Mealtime can be bonding time if you allow them to set the tone.
- Some cats are *"social eaters"* who want company during meals.

Creating Positive Feeding Experiences

What Works in Our House:

- Consistent meal times (Bengals love routine).
- Clean bowls for every meal.
- Quiet eating areas free from competition.
- Respecting individual preferences, such as Edan's social eating versus Stormy's more focused approach.

Troubleshooting Common Feeding Challenges

The Picky Eater Phase

When Bengals Become Food Critics:

- Offer variety but stick to high-quality ingredients.
- Warm wet food slightly to enhance aroma.
- Don't give in to manipulation (though its easier said than done).
- Ensure medical issues aren't causing appetite changes.

The "Inhaler" Problem

When Bengals Eat Too Fast:

- Use puzzle feeders to slow consumption.
- Split meals into smaller, more frequent portions.
- Place obstacles in food bowls to encourage slower eating.

If eating problems continue or get worse, consult your veterinarian. Sometimes behavioral eating issues signal underlying health problems.

Activity: Bengal Food Diary

Track your Bengal's eating patterns for two weeks:

- Note favorite foods, rejected meals, and eating behaviors.
- Record energy levels, coat condition, and litter box changes.
- Document any digestive upsets or unusual behaviors.
- Use this information to optimize their diet.

Tip: When testing new diets, always note changes in energy, health, and stool, and consult your vet before switching to a raw or home-prepared option.

Edan's Perspective:

"Food is serious business that demands proper presentation, the right timing, and preferably an audience to enjoy my dining performance. If you bring out the good stuff, fresh meat with a sprinkle of those mysterious powders, I'll even sing my appreciation song. But serve me boring kibble when I'm expecting gourmet, and you'll hear about it."

Stormy's Perspective:

"I'm pretty easygoing about food as long as it tastes good and arrives on schedule. Raw meat is exciting, wet food is comforting, and dry food works fine for midnight snacks. Just don't change my routine without warning, consistency is key to happiness."

Final Thoughts

Feeding your Bengal properly involves more than just providing nutrition; it's about understanding their individual tastes, keeping them healthy, and often sharing the social joy of mealtimes. Whether you opt for raw, commercial, or mixed feeding, the most important thing is to find what fits both your lifestyle and your Bengal's unique needs.

What surprised me most was discovering how much personality Bengals bring to mealtime. From Edan's dining performances to Stormy's quiet appreciation, feeding time became another way to understand and bond with them.

Begin with high-quality ingredients, observe your Bengal's responses, and be willing to make adjustments as necessary. Every Bengal is different, and discovering their ideal diet often requires patience, careful observation, and sometimes accepting that your discerning cat has developed very specific culinary preferences.

Remember: When in doubt, consult your veterinarian. They can offer professional advice tailored to your Bengal's specific health needs and life stage.

Chapter 8
Health Monitoring & Veterinary Care

The first time Stormy visited the vet, he approached it like a diplomatic mission. While Edan would have provided running commentary on every aspect of the experience, Stormy strolled out of his carrier, inspected the exam table thoroughly, and settled down as if he'd booked a spa appointment. The vet was completely charmed by his calm curiosity, and Stormy rewarded her professionalism with a slow blink and a gentle headbutt.

"This taught me that Bengals handle veterinary visits as uniquely as their personalities suggest. Edan approaches vet visits like a royal inspection; she wants to examine every surface, approve the facilities, and offer detailed commentary throughout. Stormy prefers a diplomatic style, staying calm but alert while carefully assessing the veterinary staff's competence through strategic positioning and slow blinks. Understanding your Bengal's approach to new situations helps you prepare for vet visits and work with their personality rather than against it."

That first appointment taught me how important it is to make health routines as stress-free as possible for both the cat and the owner. Now, every vet visit includes Stormy's favorite

CHAPTER 8
HEALTH MONITORING & VETERINARY CARE

blanket, treats, and plenty of patience for his signature slow-motion exit from the carrier.

Making Carriers Work for Bengals

If there's one piece of vet gear that's truly worth the investment, it's a sturdy carrier with multiple doors, extra points for a top-opening design! Bengals are quite inventive when it comes to escaping, so a well-designed carrier isn't just about safe transport; it also makes vet visits less stressful.

A top-door carrier is popular among veterinarians for good reason! Kelly, the veterinarian, who has seen her fair share of clever and anxious cats, swears by carriers that open from the top and sides. This design allows the vet to gently reach in for routine checks, vaccinations, or nail trims; no need to force a reluctant Bengal out, kicking and *"singing the song of their people."*

Kelly once shared a great example: one of her elderly clients brings her nervous cat for nail trims, and Kelly can access the front paws from the front door and the back paws from the rear, all while the cat stays safely inside the carrier.

The result? Less drama, more purrs, and neatly trimmed nails without a single flinch. Think of the top door as a personal *"stage door"* for both Edan's gourmet critiques and Stormy's diplomatic inspections, enter or exit at your Bengal's preferred pace.

Understanding Bengal-Specific Health Considerations

Bengals are generally strong, athletic cats, but their wild ancestry means they have some unique health concerns that responsible owners should be aware of.

Important note: *I'm sharing what I've learned through research and experience but always consult your veterinarian for professional medical advice. I'm a Bengal owner, not a veterinary professional.*

Hereditary Health Issues: What Every Owner Should Know

- **Hypertrophic Cardiomyopathy (HCM):** This heart condition, where the heart muscle thickens, is the most common heart disease in cats. Bengals may not show symptoms until the disease progresses, which is why annual heart screenings are crucial as they get older. The best way to diagnose and monitor this condition is through an ultrasound called an echocardiogram performed by a veterinary cardiologist. Annual screenings for Bengals are recommended as they age.

- **Progressive Retinal Atrophy (PRA):** This genetic eye condition leads to gradual vision loss. Early signs include trouble seeing in low light or bumping into objects in familiar spaces. Vision changes warrant a visit to a veterinary ophthalmologist, the eye specialist for cats, for proper diagnosis and treatment.

- **Pyruvate Kinase Deficiency (PK Def):** This hereditary condition can lead to anemia. Symptoms include pale gums, tiredness, and decreased appetite. While considered a possibility in Bengals, some vets aren't as familiar with this rare condition, and in many areas, specialized testing isn't routine. Expect to treat anemia symptoms with your regular vet if needed.

- **Flat-Chested Kitten Syndrome:** Rare in Bengals, but if you notice a kitten with a flattened chest or breathing difficulty, see your vet immediately.

What I learned from our experience: Reputable breeders screen for these conditions and provide health testing results. If you're adopting, ask about any known health history and plan for regular senior health check-ups.

Checklist: Hereditary Health Monitoring

- Request genetic testing results from your breeder or rescue.
- Schedule annual vet visits, including heart and eye checks.
- Keep a monthly log of appetite, weight, and behavior changes.

Hereditary Health Checklist				
Health Issue	When to Screen	Symptons to Watch For	Last Check	Notes
HCM (Hypertrophic Cardiomyopathy)	Yearly (from age 2+)	Heavy or rapid breathing, fainting, lethargy		
PRA (Progressive Retinal Atrophy)	Between 1–4 years old	Bumping into things, night vision loss		
PK Def (Pyruvate Kinase Deficiency)	From 6 months old	Pale gums, sluggishness, low energy		
Flat-Chested Kitten Syndrome	As a kitten	Odd chest shape, difficulty breathing		

If possible, keep a hard copy of your Bengal's medical records along with a digital file. Phones are convenient, but batteries die, or service can be nonexistent in waiting rooms!

Building Your Veterinary Support Team

It was nearly midnight when Edan managed to swallow a shoelace during a game of *"sock soccer."* Stormy watched, wide-eyed, as I desperately searched for the vet's number, showing that even the most prepared Bengal parent can freeze in an emergency. That night, having the right support info right next to the phone made all the difference.

CHAPTER 8
HEALTH MONITORING & VETERINARY CARE

Finding the Right Veterinary Care

What Worked for Us:

- Found a vet experienced with active, intelligent cat breeds.
- Established a relationship before any emergencies arose.
- Asked about after-hours emergency protocols during our first visit.
- Created a Bengal health file with all records in one place.

The Insurance Reality: Timing Matters

"The universe has a sense of humor about pet insurance timing. The day after your waiting period ends, your Bengal will show perfect health. The day before? That's when they'll discover their calling as a dietary explorer, specializing in non-food items."

But on a serious note, when I took Stormy in for his welcome checkup, the vet mentioned a heart murmur, not uncommon in Bengals and often harmless. Since this happened during our insurance waiting period, it became a *"pre-existing condition"* that would never be covered, even with future policies.

What I Learned About Pet Insurance:

- **Waiting periods matter**: Typically, 30-90 days for illness coverage.
- **Timing is everything**: Start insurance before your first vet visit, not after.
- **Pre-existing conditions stick**: Even switching insurers won't help.
- **Read the fine print:** Know your policy's breed-specific exclusions.

What to Look for in a Policy:

- Coverage for accidents, illnesses, and hereditary conditions (like HCM).
- Clear understanding of exclusions and age limits.
- Reasonable reimbursement percentages and deductibles.
- International coverage if you travel.

This is my experience with Australian insurance policies. Coverage varies greatly by country and provider, so explore options in your area.

Tips for New Bengal Owners:

- Start insurance before the first vet visit.
- Ask direct questions about breed-specific coverage.
- Keep detailed records of all health information.

Chapter 8
Health Monitoring & Veterinary Care

Remember: even mild heart murmurs require ongoing monitoring.

Building Positive Veterinary Relationships: The Partnership Approach

Building a strong relationship with your veterinary team benefits everyone, especially your Bengal. Bengals often need more detailed explanations of their behavior and energy levels than typical house cats, so clear, open communication is crucial. When scheduling appointments, mention that you have a Bengal; this helps staff prepare for an active, intelligent cat who may require extra patience during examinations.

Remember that veterinary nurses and support staff serve as your pet's advocates, not as the ones controlling financial policies. They have chosen this profession out of a genuine concern for animal welfare and often work long, emotionally demanding hours. When it comes to treatment costs or insurance questions, it's best to speak with practice managers instead of clinical staff. Your veterinary team aims to provide the best care for your Bengal; working together respectfully helps achieve the best results for everyone. A simple *"thank you"* to the nurse holding your restless Bengal during vaccinations can significantly strengthen the supportive relationship, making future visits more comfortable for you and your cat.

When Community and Veterinary Care Make All the Difference: Edan's Survival Story

Six weeks after moving to our rural property, Edan demonstrated her door-opening skills by escaping at 4:30 PM on a winter Thursday, without her GPS tracker. In our new country setting, surrounded by busy country roads and predators, an escaped Bengal faced real danger.

For four days, an incredible community response unfolded. Neighbors I'd never met joined search parties organized by my real estate agent, Danielle. The local wildlife officer provided guidance about predator patterns. Beautiful neighbors Ness and Andrew left flowers at our fence post, what we call *"the trading post,"* where country neighbors leave goodies for each other, with notes of support.

A local woman responded to my Facebook post with car camera footage showing a motionless cat beside the road. Her daughter had said, *"Look, that cat looks like a leopard."* We raced to the location but found only Edan's collar. I accepted she was gone, grieving through the weekend while caring for kitten Stormy.

On Monday morning, as I was heading out to start work, I heard a small voice coming from under the house. Dismissing it as a grief-induced hallucination, I continued with my routine. When I heard it again, I investigated and saw Edan's little head emerging from beneath the foundation. I collapsed in tears, holding her against me, then stumbled inside, sobbing

Chapter 8
Health Monitoring & Veterinary Care

incoherently to my husband, who initially thought I was carrying her lifeless body.

Our local veterinarian stayed in contact during the search. When I called that Monday morning, she opened her clinic immediately, well before her regular hours. The examination showed a sprained leg, bloodied eye and chin, and swelling, but nothing life-threatening. How Edan survived four winter nights in unfamiliar territory, found her way home to a property she'd known for only six weeks, and endured below-zero temperatures remains a mystery.

This experience taught me that veterinary and community relationships aren't just about routine care; they can become lifelines in emergencies. Our local veterinarian's willingness to open early, neighbors who spent their weekend searching for a cat they'd never met, and the network that rallied around our crisis-built bonds that last today. Building these relationships before you need them isn't just practical, it's crucial.

Emergency Preparedness: When Crisis Strikes

Bengal emergencies seem to follow Murphy's Law perfectly; they happen at midnight, on holidays, or right after you've drained your emergency fund on something sensible like rent. Edan once scheduled her shoelace-swallowing adventure for 11:47 PM on Christmas Eve, because apparently, regular Tuesday emergencies don't have enough drama. Stormy watched, wide-eyed, as I frantically searched for the vet's number, proof that even the most prepared Bengal parent can freeze in a crisis. That night, having the right support information posted on the fridge made all the difference.

Essential Emergency Information

Keep This Information Easily Accessible:

- Primary vet contact and after-hours number.
- Nearest 24-hour emergency clinic with address.
- Animal poison control hotline for your country.
- Bengal's microchip number and basic health information.

Poison & Emergency Quick Reference Table

Note: These numbers and services may change. Always verify with your local vet or vet college for the latest animal emergency contacts. If you're unsure, contact your regular veterinarian quickly or search for *"emergency vet in your area."*

What to Have Ready for Emergency Calls

Before you call in a panic, gather:

- Your Bengal's current weight and age.
- Clear description of symptoms and timeline.
- List of any medications or recent changes.
- Transport plan (carrier ready, route to emergency clinic).

CHAPTER 8
HEALTH MONITORING & VETERINARY CARE

Poison & Emergency Quick Reference Table

Country	Hotline Name	Phone Number / Contact	Hours	Notes
United States	ASPCA Animal Poison Control Center	(888) 426-4435	24/7	Fees may apply
United States	Pet Poison Helpline	(855) 764-7661	24/7	Fees may apply
United Kingdom	Animal Poison Line (VPIS, for owners)	01202 509000	24/7	£35–£45/call, for pet owners
New Zealand	NZ National Poisons Centre	0800 764 766	24/7	General poisoning; ask for animal help
Australia	Australian Animal Poisons Centre	1300 869 738	24/7	Free for pet owners; vet consults may incur a fee
Canada	Pet Poison Helpline (North America)	(855) 764-7661	24/7	Fees may apply, serves Canada & USA

Example Table: Essential Support Contacts

Service	Name / Number	Location	Hours
Main Vet Clinic	[Your Local Clinic Name]	[Address]	[Hours]
After-Hours Emergency Vet	[Emergency Vet Service]	[Address]	24/7
Cat-Only Clinic	[Cat Clinic]	[Address]	[Hours]
National Animal Poisons	1300 869 738 (Australia example)	Hotline	24/7
Backup Clinic	[Backup Vet Name]	[Address]	[Hours]

Fill this out before bringing your Bengal home, and tape it to your fridge. Add stickers or drawings; Edan recommends a paw print for each place that hands out treats.

Access your printable resources using the QR code on page 2.

Health Crisis Recognition & First Aid

Recognizing Bengal Health "Red Flags"

Bengals hide illness remarkably well; it's a survival instinct from their wild heritage. Watch for:

- Sudden lethargy or collapse.
- Rapid breathing or open-mouth panting.
- Persistent vomiting or diarrhea.
- Blood in urine or stool.
- Sudden hiding or behavior changes.

If you observe any of these signs, contact your vet promptly. Trust your instincts; you know your cat better than anyone

Bengal First Aid Kit Essentials

What to Keep on Hand:

- Sterile gauze pads and medical tape.
- Digital thermometer and lubricant.
- Saline solution for eye/wound flushing.
- Emergency vet and poison control contact numbers.
- Clean towels and slip lead for safe transport.
- Pet carrier (always kept ready).

CHAPTER 8
HEALTH MONITORING & VETERINARY CARE

Vet's Warning on Choking & Swallowing Objects

Sometimes, even the bravest Bengal owner needs to pause before jumping in. If you see something sharp (like a sewing needle or string with thread) in your cat's mouth, don't try to pull it out yourself! Pulling could cause more harm than good, especially if the string or object has already been swallowed. Think of it as an unwanted game of tug-of-war with your Bengal's insides. Always go straight to the vet for anything sharp, long, or suspicious in their mouth or throat.

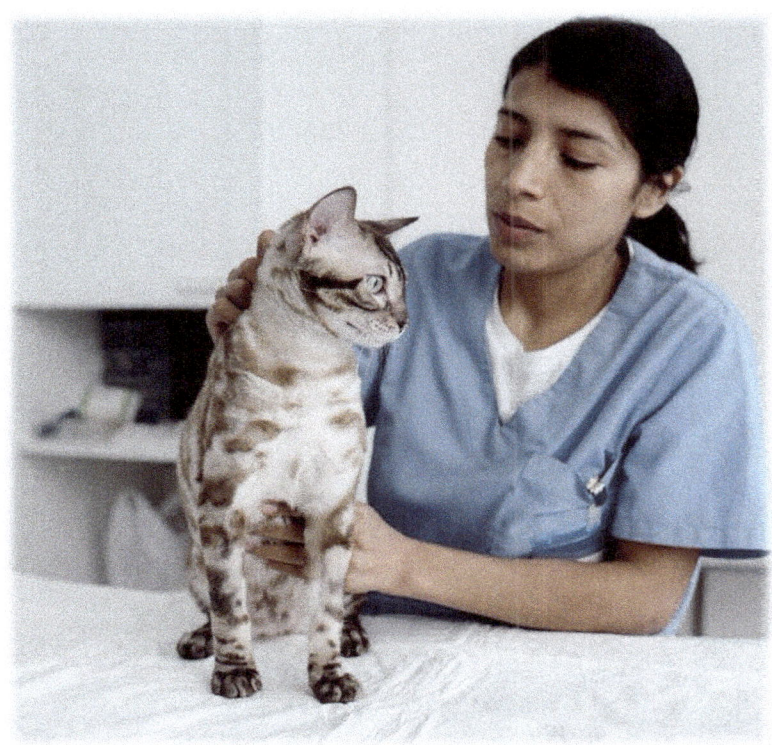

Essential First Aid Steps

For Common Emergencies:

- **Bleeding:** Press a clean cloth firmly on the wound, add layers if necessary, and go to the vet.
- **Choking:** If you see visible objects and it's safe to remove, use tweezers (never fingers), taking extra care to push it deeper. Never try to remove sharp items yourself; go straight to a vet for anything dangerous or if the object doesn't come out quickly.
- **Poisoning:** Move the cat from the source, call poison control immediately, and bring the substance packaging.
- **Seizures:** Clear the area, don't restrain, time the seizure, and keep warm and quiet afterwards.

Remember: First aid is about stabilizing until you can get professional veterinary care.

Ongoing Health Monitoring

Monthly Health Checks:

What I Track for Edan and Stormy:

- Weight and body condition changes.
- Appetite, drinking, and litter box habits.
- Energy levels and play preferences.
- Any physical changes or behavioral shifts.

Stress Recognition and Management

Bengals can show stress in subtle ways:

- Overgrooming or thinning fur.
- Hiding or skipping meals.
- Uncharacteristic irritability.
- Sudden litter box issues.

Stress-Busting Strategies:

- Conduct a *"stress audit"* for recent household changes
- Use calming pheromone diffusers.
- Maintain regular play sessions.
- Provide quiet hideouts and escape routes.

Activity: Health Record Organization

Create a comprehensive health tracking system:

- Digital folder or physical binder for all records.
- Monthly weight and behavior logs.
- Vaccination schedules and reminders.
- Emergency contact updates.

Stormy: Every heartbeat is an adventure; make each one count!

A phone app or a notes file is great, unless you're deep in the bush with Edan and Stormy and can't get a signal, or need to pass info to the vet while juggling an anxious Bengal with both hands. Always keep a hard copy in your Bengal health binder, with all key info printed and ready to grab. When chaos strikes, paper beats pixels every time.

Chapter 8
Health Monitoring & Veterinary Care

Edan's Perspective:

"Health monitoring should include regular assessment of treat quality, nap comfort levels, and human response time to my requests. If you're going to poke and prod during vet visits, excellent treats are mandatory compensation."

Stormy's Perspective:

"I prefer a gentle approach to healthcare, calm environments, patient handling, familiar blankets, and my records nearby. A little extra attention and some favorite treats make everything easier for everyone involved."

Final Thoughts

Bengal health care blends routine preventive measures with understanding your individual needs and your cat's normal patterns. The most important thing you can do is build relationships with qualified veterinary professionals before you need them and learn to recognize what's normal for your specific Bengal.

What I've learned through experience: good health care relies on partnership, between you and your vet, and between you and your Bengal. The better you understand your cat's normal behavior and needs, the better you'll be able to advocate for their health and well-being.

Remember that every Bengal is unique, and health needs change with age and circumstances. Stay observant, ask questions, and don't hesitate to seek professional guidance when something doesn't seem right.

"While we've discussed the overall picture of Bengal health monitoring, there's one daily health indicator that needs special focus: litter box habits. Changes in bathroom behavior frequently indicate health problems before other signs show up, making litter box management both a comfort and health priority."

Chapter 9
Litter Box Mastery

Bengals are famously particular about their bathroom facilities, and for good reasons. A clean, properly sized litter box isn't just a convenience, it's crucial for their health, happiness, and household harmony. Set it up correctly, and your Bengal will reward you with consistent good habits. Get it wrong, and you'll quickly notice their dissatisfaction.

What I learned from living with two Bengals: litter box standards are non-negotiable. They have opinions on everything from box size to litter texture, and they're not shy about sharing those opinions.

Choosing the Right Litter Box: Size Matters

Bengals are energetic cats that need lots of space to roam freely. Small, covered boxes suitable for many cats are not ideal for Bengals.

What Actually Works

Size Guidelines That Work:

- **Length:** At least 1.5 times your Bengal's body length from nose to tail.
- **Width**: Wide enough for comfortable turning and positioning.

- **Height:** High sides to contain enthusiastic digging, but accessible entry.

My Experience with Box Types:

- **Open boxes:** Most Bengals prefer these for visibility and airflow.
- **High-sided boxes:** Essential for vigorous diggers like Stormy.
- **Covered boxes:** Some cats love privacy, others feel trapped, test carefully.

Stormy treats his litter box like a construction project, digging elaborate preparations before doing his business. High-sided boxes became necessary after discovering litter spread in a three-foot radius around standard boxes.

Many Bengal owners have achieved success with various litter box styles and brands. Here are some popular options to help you begin your search; remember, what works for one cat might not work for another.

Bengal Owners Litter Box Styles		
Brand / Model	Features	Notes
Litter-Robot	Self-cleaning, large, open design	Great for multi-cat homes
Catit Jumbo Hooded	Spacious, covered, carbon filter	Good for privacy-loving Bengals
Modkat XL	High sides, top or front entry	Stylish, easy to clean
PetSafe ScoopFree	Self-cleaning, disposable trays	Low maintenance, less odor

Litter Selection: The Texture Test

Bengals have sensitive paws and strong preferences for litter texture. What works for other cats may be rejected completely by a picky Bengal.

What I've Learned Through Trial and Error

Generally Successful Options:

- Unscented clumping clay (most Bengals approve).
- Fine-grain textures that don't stick to paws.
- Natural litters like corn or wheat (gradual introduction recommended).

Usually Rejected Options:

- Heavily scented litters (overpowering to sensitive noses).
- Dusty clay that irritates the respiratory system.
- Large-grain litters that feel uncomfortable on paws.

If your Bengal suddenly avoids the litter box, trying a different litter texture is often the first troubleshooting step before assuming behavioral issues.

Placement Strategy: Location Matters

The Golden Rules of Litter Box Placement

What Works in Our House:

- Quiet, low-traffic areas where cats feel secure.
- Multiple locations to prevent resource competition.
- Easy access but away from food and water areas.
- Good ventilation without being drafty.

What Doesn't Work:

- Next to noisy appliances (washing machines, water heaters).
- High-traffic hallways where cats feel exposed.
- Basement corners that feel isolated or threatening.
- Areas where cats can be cornered or surprised.

With two Bengals, we follow the *"one box per cat plus one extra"* rule, placing them in different areas to prevent territorial disputes.

Multi-Cat Dynamics: Managing Bengal Personalities

What I Learned from Edan and Stormy

When Stormy joined our household, I noticed how litter box territories formed. Interestingly, they developed their own usage patterns without any competition. Edan prefers the box in the quiet study, while Stormy uses the one in the laundry room.

Multi-Bengal Success Strategies:

- Multiple boxes in different locations.
- Different litter types, if cats have preferences.
- Separate cleaning schedules to prevent scent competition.
- Watching for signs of resource guarding or avoidance.

Step-by-Step Litter Training

Edan learned quickly, especially when I praised her for using the box and keeping the area around it spotless. She's now my *"clean queen,"* always letting me know if something's not up to her standards.

Whether you're starting with a kitten or retraining an adult, patience is key.

1. **Introduce the box:** Place your Bengal in the box after meals and naps.
2. **Praise and reward:** Gentle encouragement (and the occasional treat) helps reinforce good habits.
3. **Never punish:** If there's an accident, clean it up quietly and try again. Punishment only causes anxiety and sneaky behavior.

This playful Bengal's litter box audit: step one, redecorate with the finest toilet roll money can buy!

CHAPTER 9
LITTER BOX MASTERY

Activity: Litter Box Success Tracker

Create a simple chart to log your Bengal's litter box habits for two weeks. Include:

- Date and time.
- Which box was used?
- Any accidents or unusual behavior.
- Notes on cleanliness or changes.

Reflect on patterns. Do accidents occur after missed cleanings or when introducing new litter? Adjust routines as needed.

Bengal Litter Training Tracker

Date	Location	Success?	Notes / Accidents
Oct 8, 2025	Laundry Room	Yes	Used box after breakfast
Oct 7, 2025	Living Room	No	Accident on rug

Troubleshooting: When Things Go Wrong

Medical Issues First

When to Call the Vet:

- Sudden avoidance of previously accepted boxes.
- Straining, blood in urine, or frequent small amounts.
- Excessive digging or unusual vocalizations in the box.
- Any dramatic change in litter box habits.

Always rule out medical causes before assuming behavioral problems. Urinary issues can be serious and need prompt veterinary care.

Environmental Problem-Solving

Common Issues and Solutions I've Discovered:

Box Cleanliness:

- Scoop at least twice daily (non-negotiable with Bengals).
- Complete litter changes weekly.
- Monthly deep cleaning with unscented soap.

Location Problems:

- Move boxes to quieter, more private locations.
- Ensure easy access from multiple directions.
- Remove any new obstacles or stressors from near boxes.

Litter Texture Issues:

- Gradual transitions when changing litter types.
- Offer choice by providing different litters in separate boxes.
- Return to previously successful options if problems arise.

Chapter 9
Litter Box Mastery

Cleanliness Routines That Actually Work

Daily Maintenance

The Twice-Daily Scoop Routine: Morning scooping becomes part of my coffee preparation routine, while evening scooping occurs during dinner prep. This consistency keeps both cats happy and prevents odor buildup.

What Makes Cleaning Easier:

- High-quality scooping tools with comfortable grips.
- Odor-controlling litter that clumps well.
- Convenient waste disposal system near boxes.
- Rubber mats to catch scattered litter.

Weekly Deep Cleaning

The Complete Reset:

- Empty the boxes entirely and wash with mild soap.
- Check for scratches or damage that might harbor bacteria.
- Replace litter completely rather than topping off.
- Clean surrounding areas, including walls and floors.

I learned this thorough approach after discovering that Bengal noses are extremely sensitive to lingering odors that humans might not even notice.

Activity: Litter Box Assessment

Weekly Box Evaluation:

- Check that the box size is adequate as your Bengal grows.
- Note any changes in usage patterns or preferences.
- Evaluate cleanliness standards and adjust the schedule if needed.
- Monitor for any signs of avoidance or discomfort.

Monthly Setup Review:

- Assess the boxes' locations for any environmental changes.
- Consider whether additional boxes might reduce competition.
- Evaluate litter type satisfaction based on usage patterns.
- Update cleaning supplies and replacement schedule.

Chapter 9
Litter Box Mastery

Edan's Perspective:

"My bathroom standards are quite reasonable: spotless conditions, appropriate privacy, and prompt cleanup service. If you meet these simple requirements, I'll continue to use the designated facilities. Fail to meet my standards, and I'll be forced to find alternative arrangements that you probably won't like."

Stormy's Perspective:

"I prefer to take my time with bathroom routines, proper setup, enough space to move around, and no interruptions during essential tasks. A clean, quiet space in a secure location meets all my needs. Rush me or give me subpar facilities, and we'll have to renegotiate this arrangement."

Final Thoughts

Litter box success with Bengals depends on understanding their standards and maintaining consistent care routines. They're not being difficult; they're expressing valid preferences for cleanliness, comfort, and security.

What surprised me most was discovering how much personality Bengals show in every part of their daily routines, including bathroom habits. Respecting their preferences and upholding high standards builds a foundation for household harmony.

Investing in proper boxes, quality litter, and regular upkeep pays off in cat happiness and household cleanliness. When you meet Bengal bathroom standards, you'll develop good habits and cats that feel safe and comfortable in their environment.

Remember: Sudden changes in litter box behavior often indicate health problems or environmental stressors. Stay observant, uphold high standards, and consult your veterinarian if issues continue despite environmental adjustments.

Chapter 10
Grooming & daily care

Every Bengal cat is a moving masterpiece, shimmering, spotted, and always ready for the camera. But even the most stunning coat needs regular human help to stay at its best. Think of grooming as spa time for your wild child, though whether they enjoy the pampering depends entirely on their personality and your approach.

Brushing: Maintaining That Famous Bengal Glitter

Bengals have short, dense coats that often shimmer with what's called *"glitter,"* tiny hollow hair tips that reflect light. Although they naturally shed less than fluffier breeds, regular brushing keeps their fur shiny, reduces hairballs, and provides valuable bonding time.

What I've learned from grooming Edan and Stormy: every Bengal has unique tolerance levels and preferences. The key is to work with their personality, not against it.

"Spa day: the only time a Bengal voluntarily stays still for more than thirty seconds. Note the strategic positioning, paws tucked, eyes closed, but ears still on high alert for the treat jar opening three rooms away. Professional grooming tip: the secret to Bengal cooperation is convincing them the spa treatment was their idea in the first place."

What Actually Works in Practice

Frequency That Works for Us:

- **Regular maintenance:** Once or twice weekly for most Bengals.
- **Seasonal adjustment:** More frequent brushing during spring and fall shedding periods.
- **Individual variation:** Edan loves brief daily brushing sessions; Stormy prefers shorter, more frequent grooming.

Tools That Pass Bengal Approval:

- **Rubber grooming mitts:** Feel like a massage, effective for loose hair removal.
- **Fine-toothed metal combs:** Perfect for detail work and catching missed spots.
- **Soft bristle brushes:** Gentle finishing touches that most cats enjoy.

Avoid harsh slicker brushes; Bengal skin can be surprisingly sensitive despite its tough appearance.

Making Brushing Enjoyable

- **Edan's Grooming Preferences:** She treats brushing like a royal spa experience, stretching out luxuriously and purring throughout. Her secret: I start with gentle strokes along her back, following the direction of her fur, then gradually move to areas she's less enthusiastic about.
- **Stormy's Approach:** He prefers shorter sessions with more treats. I've learned to read his body language. When his tail twitches, it's time to end the session on a good note.

The main point: grooming should never turn into a wrestling match. If your Bengal isn't enjoying it, review your technique, tools, or timing.

Understanding these personality differences taught me that successful Bengal grooming requires tailoring your approach to your individual cat's temperament and tolerance levels. Edan's confidence means she'll communicate clearly when something feels good (luxurious stretching and purring) versus when I'm pushing her limits (slight tension in her posture). Stormy's more cautious nature means I need to watch for subtler signals; a slight tail twitch or shift in position tells me it's time to offer treats and praise before continuing.

What I've learned about personality-based grooming approaches:

For confident, social Bengals (like Edan):

- Longer sessions work well when they're in the mood.
- They'll clearly communicate preferences and boundaries.
- Often enjoy grooming as social bonding time.
- May seek out grooming sessions when they want attention.

For cautious, methodical Bengals (like Stormy):

- Shorter, more frequent sessions prevent overwhelming them.
- Treats and praise help build positive associations.
- Respect their *"finished"* signals immediately.
- Consistency in technique and timing builds trust.

The key is learning to understand your specific Bengal's communication style and working with their personality instead of expecting them to adapt to your preferred grooming schedule. Some Bengals express their grooming preferences loudly, while others communicate through subtle body language cues. Both approaches are normal; your job is to become fluent in your cat's unique way of communicating.

Bathing: When Water Meets Bengal Opinions

Bengals have a well-known relationship with water; they're fascinated by it until you actually try to give them a bath. Some will jump into bathtubs willingly; others act like you've suggested swimming with sharks.

When Bathing is Actually Necessary

Situations That Require Baths:

- Getting into something sticky or dirty during adventures.
- Preparing for cat shows (if you're into that scene).
- Medical conditions requiring medicated shampoos.
- Occasional maintenance for indoor cats who can't groom effectively.

How Often: Only when genuinely necessary. Most Bengals remain remarkably clean through regular brushing and their own grooming efforts.

The Bathing Strategy That Works

What I've Learned Through Experience:

- **Preparation is everything:** Lukewarm water, cat-safe shampoo, thick towels ready.
- **Gradual introduction:** Wet paws first, then gradually work up to full body.
- **Avoid the face and ears:** These areas rarely need washing, and cats hate water in sensitive areas.

Chapter 10
Grooming & Daily Care

- **Quick and efficient:** The faster you work, the less stress for everyone involved.
- **Post-bath comfort:** Immediate towel burrito and treats for forgiveness.

Edan rates baths 3/10 for the experience but 10/10 for the towel burrito afterward. I consider this a grooming win.

Use only lukewarm water and never leave cats unattended near standing water. Provide non-slip surfaces for safety.

"You said, 'play with water,' not 'become the water!'"

205

Nail Care: The Great Claw Debate

Bengal claws serve several key functions: climbing, safely descending from heights, marking territory, and relieving stress. Whether to trim them or not mainly depends on your individual Bengal's lifestyle and your household setup.

When to Trim vs. When to Leave Natural

- **Our Approach with Supervised Outdoor Time:** Since Edan and Stormy spend supervised time climbing trees and exploring outdoors, I don't trim their nails. They need full claw functionality for safe tree climbing and confident outdoor exploration.
- **For Indoor-Only Bengals:** Regular trimming every 2-4 weeks may be needed to prevent furniture damage and accidental scratches during play.

Nail Trimming Basics (For Those Who Choose This Route)

Tools and Techniques:

- Cat-specific nail clippers or rounded human nail scissors.
- Styptic powder for minor accidents.
- Trim only the sharp white tips, never the pink quick.
- One paw per session is perfectly acceptable for resistant cats.

Every Bengal cat is unique; some tolerate nail trims easily, while others need creative bribery and patience'

CHAPTER 10
GROOMING & DAILY CARE

Edan, breathtaking and fully in her element; there's nothing more beautiful than a Bengal queen surveying her kingdom from the treetops!

Edan is proving that in the Bengal world, the sky isn't the limit; it's just the beginning!

Always supervise tree climbing and make sure cats keep their claws for safe descent. Never try to *"rescue"* a confident climber; they understand their limits better than we do.

Dental Care: Beyond Pretty Smiles

Dental health greatly affects overall well-being, making tooth care a vital part of maintenance rather than just cosmetic grooming.

What Actually Works for Busy Owners

Ideal Routine:

- Brush teeth 2-3 times weekly with cat-safe toothpaste.
- Use finger brushes or soft-bristled cat toothbrushes.
- Never use human toothpaste (toxic to cats).

Reality-Based Alternatives:

- Dental treats and toys designed for plaque control.
- Adding dental enzymes to food or water (with vet approval).
- Regular professional cleanings during veterinary visits.

Warning Signs to Watch For:

- Bad breath, red or swollen gums, and difficulty eating.
- Pawing at the face or reluctance to eat hard foods.
- Visible tartar buildup or loose teeth.

If dental issues arise, seeking professional veterinary care is crucial as I am sharing maintenance tips, not medical treatment advice.

Ear Care: Gentle Maintenance

Bengal ears usually stay clean through natural grooming, but occasional gentle cleaning helps prevent problems and allows you to check for issues.

When Ear Cleaning is Helpful

Normal Maintenance Situations:

- Visible dirt or wax buildup.
- After outdoor adventures in dusty environments.
- As part of a regular health monitoring routine.

What Works for Us:

- Soft cotton balls with vet-approved ear cleaner.
- Clean only what you can see—never probe deep into ear canals.
- Watch for signs of irritation, infection, or unusual odors.

When to Call the Vet:

- Dark, coffee-ground-like debris (possible ear mites).
- Red, swollen, or painful-looking ears.
- Strong odors or discharge.
- Head shaking or excessive scratching at the ears.

Ear problems can worsen rapidly, so it's usually best to seek professional evaluation when issues occur

Clean ears, sharp hearing; nothing escapes the Bengal patrol!

Creating Grooming Routines That Work

The Weekly Grooming Schedule That Actually Happens

What Works in Our House:

- **Monday:** Quick brush and nail check.
- **Wednesday:** Thorough brushing and ear inspection.
- **Friday:** Dental care and overall health assessment.
- **As needed:** Baths, nail trims, or extra brushing during shedding season.

Making it Sustainable:

- Keep sessions short and positive.
- Have treats ready for cooperation.
- Stop before cats get frustrated or stressed.
- Celebrate small victories and progress.

Activity: Personal Grooming Tracker

Weekly Assessment Questions:

- Which grooming activities does your Bengal enjoy vs. tolerate, vs. dislike?
- What time of day and environmental conditions work best?

- Which tools and treats make the most significant difference in cooperation?
- Are there any health issues or changes you've noticed during grooming?

Monthly Equipment Check:

- Are brushes and combs clean and in good condition?
- Do you have appropriate dental care supplies?
- Are nail clippers sharp and safe to use?
- Is your first aid kit stocked for minor grooming accidents?

Edan's Perspective:

"Grooming is acceptable when done with proper respect for my magnificence. I expect gentle methods, good tools, and treats for my cooperation. Brush me correctly, and I'll purr in appreciation. Rush the process or use poor-quality equipment, and I'll show my displeasure clearly."

Stormy's Perspective:

"I prefer a relaxed grooming style, comfortable positions, no sudden movements, and plenty of breaks for treats and chin scratches. Make it a pleasant experience, and I'll gladly participate. If you try to force anything, we'll have to renegotiate our arrangement."

Final Thoughts

Grooming your Bengal successfully relies on understanding their individual preferences and creating positive associations with essential care routines. It's not about forcing cooperation—it's about making experiences enjoyable for both of you.

What surprised me most was realizing how much grooming could improve our relationships. When done thoughtfully, grooming time turns into bonding moments, health checks, and opportunities to show care in ways your Bengal can understand.

The key is patience, good tools, and realistic expectations. Some Bengals will enjoy elaborate grooming sessions; others prefer quick, efficient maintenance. Both methods can keep your Bengal healthy and beautiful when suited to their personality and comfort level.

Remember that grooming also offers regular chances to spot health changes, lumps, or other issues that may need veterinary attention. This preventive role makes grooming an essential part of overall Bengal care, not just for appearance.

Chapter 11
Training & Enrichment

The first time I tried clicker training with Edan, she treated it like an intriguing puzzle. She looked at the treat, then at me, then at the clicker, clearly thinking, *"You want me to do what for this snack?"* After one successful high-five, she strutted around the living room with her tail held high, convinced she had invented the trick herself. Meanwhile, Stormy watched the whole thing before deciding he'd only join in if the treat-to-effort ratio matched his standards.

What that experience taught me: Bengal training focuses less on obedience and more on stimulating their minds in ways that feel rewarding to them. They're not just performing for you; they're problem-solving alongside you.

Why Training Matters for Bengal Brains

Bengals are feline Einsteins wrapped in spotted coats. Without enough mental stimulation, they'll entertain themselves by redesigning your home in unexpected ways. Training provides structured challenges that fulfil their need for mental engagement and help you communicate more effectively with them.

CHAPTER 11
TRAINING & ENRICHMENT

The Reality of Bengal Intelligence

What Living with Smart Cats Actually Means:

- They learn your routines and anticipate your actions
- Problem-solving is entertainment, not frustration
- They remember training sessions and expect consistency
- Boredom leads to creative mischief that tests your patience.

In my experience, the most *"difficult"* Bengal behaviors usually stem from under-stimulation rather than genuine behavioral problems.

Clicker Training: Speaking the Bengal Language

Clicker training works particularly well with Bengals because it offers immediate, clear feedback that matches their intelligence. The click sound indicates the exact moment they perform the desired behavior, establishing precise communication.

"Training a Bengal is like being a personal assistant to a tiny, furry CEO who changes her mind every five minutes and pays in purrs. Edan's performance reviews include detailed critiques of treat quality, timing, and whether I've adequately celebrated her brilliance."

Getting Started: The Basics That Work

Essential Equipment:

- Clicker or consistent sound maker (I use a pen that clicks reliably)
- High-value treats that your Bengal actually wants (freeze-dried chicken works magic)
- Patience and realistic session length expectations.

First Steps That Build Success:

1. Associate the click with treats: Click, immediately offer a treat, repeat until your Bengal perks up at the click sound
2. Start simple: *"Touch"* (nose to finger), *"sit,"* or *"look"* are good beginning behaviors
3. Keep sessions short: 5 minutes is plenty for most Bengal attention spans
4. End on success: Always finish with a behavior your cat can do easily.

CHAPTER 11
TRAINING & ENRICHMENT

Advanced Training: When Your Bengal Gets Competitive

Stormy's Training Breakthrough: The day Stormy mastered *"catch the mouse"* (bringing his toy to me on command), he treated it like winning the Bengal Olympics. He carried that mouse across the room with theatrical flair, pausing for dramatic effect before dropping it at my feet and waiting for applause.

Skills That Work Well for Bengals:

- Fetch variations: Many Bengals naturally retrieve toys
- High fives and paw shakes: Appeals to their show-off tendencies
- *"Go to"* commands: Teaching them to go to specific spots on cue
- Puzzle solving: Teaching them to operate treat-dispensing toys

Every Bengal learns differently. Edan quickly picks up physical tricks; Stormy excels at problem-solving challenges that involve food rewards.

Harness Training: Adventures Beyond the Living Room

Harness training provides safe outdoor adventures for Bengals who seek environmental enrichment but need protection from traffic, predators, and getting lost.

Edan's "Fashion Forward" Adventure

The first time I tried to harness Stormy, he looked at me as if I'd suggested we go skydiving without a parachute. Meanwhile, Edan strutted around, convinced the harness was a new fashion accessory. If you're picturing a graceful stroll on day one, prepare for a comedy show instead. But with patience (and treats), even the most dramatic Bengal can become a confident explorer!

Edan's no stranger to the spotlight; she's graced the aisles modeling for Pet Stock shop and strutted her stuff for Kmart shopping. Nobody sashays quite like her when a camera's around!

Why Harness Training?

Choosing the Right Harness: Breeder-Approved Tips

Lyn Dowd of Metanoia Bengals in Richmond, Tasmania, swears by Velcro-fit harnesses for a secure, comfortable experience. Her top choice: Butterfly jackets from Etsy (made in the UK). These wrap gently around your Bengal's body, fasten with strong Velcro, and are less likely to let a determined feline wriggle free.

Why Velcro-Fit Harnesses?

- More secure: Reduces the risk of escape.
- Gentle fit: Distributes pressure evenly; no pinching or digging in.
- Easy on and off: Quick to put on, less drama for both cat and human.
- Stylish: Butterfly jackets come in fun patterns and colors.

The Step-by-Step Reality

Phase 1: Harness Introduction (Weeks 1-2)

- Leave the harness near your favorite sleeping spots
- Let your Bengal sniff, investigate, and even sleep on it
- Positive associations through treats and play near the harness

Phase 2: Fitting and Wearing (Weeks 3-4)

- Drape the harness over your Bengal without fastening (treats during this)
- Gradually fasten for very short periods with distractions (meals, play)
- Expect some dramatic flopping; this is normal adjustment behavior

Phase 3: Movement and Leash (Weeks 5-6)

- Encourage movement while wearing a harness indoors
- Attach the leash and let them drag it under supervision
- Practice gentle guidance with treats, never pulling or forcing

Phase 4: Outdoor Adventures (Week 7+)

- Start in secure, quiet areas like enclosed courtyards
- Let your Bengal set the exploration pace initially
- Build confidence through positive experiences

When Harness Training Doesn't Work

Accepting Individual Preferences: Not every Bengal will enjoy harness walks, and that's perfectly normal. Some cats prefer watching the world from cozy indoor perches rather than going outside directly.

Signs to Respect:

- Continued stress or fear despite gradual introduction
- Complete refusal to move while wearing a harness
- Aggressive attempts to remove the harness.

If your Bengal clearly dislikes harness training, try enriching their indoor environment instead. Window perches, catios, or supervised porch time could be better options.

Activity: Harness Training Progress Chart

Create a straightforward chart to monitor your Bengal's progress through each phase. Record daily comfort levels, breakthrough moments, and setbacks. Celebrate every milestone (and every dramatic flop)!

Harness Training Progress Chart

Day	Milestone	Notes
Day 1	Sniffed harness?	
Day 2	Wore harness for 1 minute?	
Day 3	Walked with harness indoors?	
Day 4	Tried leash indoors?	
Day 5+	First outdoor adventure?	

Celebrate every milestone (and every dramatic flop)!

Harness Training Tips for Success:

- Try a Velcro-fit Butterfly jacket from Etsy for comfort and security
- Snap a photo of your Bengal in their harness; bonus points for creative patterns!
- Track your Bengal's comfort level each day with the progress chart
- Use high-value treats to make harness time a positive experience

Harness training is a journey, not a sprint. With patience, laughter, and a secure Velcro-fit harness, your Bengal will soon be strutting their stuff like a mini jungle explorer. Remember: every Bengal is unique, so celebrate the little wins and enjoy the adventure together.

Fashion, function, and a feline attitude are all important factors to consider. Metanoia Frog Prince in his Butterfly Jacket Harness says, 'If you're going to walk, do it with flair!'

Make sure the harness fits securely; you should be able to fit two fingers under it. Never leave cats unattended while they are wearing harnesses.

CHAPTER 11
TRAINING & ENRICHMENT

Enrichment: Keeping Bengal Minds Busy

DIY Solutions That Actually Work

Cardboard Box Engineering: Stormy and Edan have shown me that pricey toys often can't match a well-crafted cardboard box setup. Cut holes for hide-and-seek games, build tunnels, or simply keep boxes in rotation for exploration.

Stormy always arrives first to inspect every package, turning boxes into fortresses and racetracks. Edan is all about the paper bags, rustling and popping her head out like a hide-and-seek champion. Sometimes, the best toys are the simplest!

Always remove handles from paper bags before play to prevent strangulation hazards.

If there's a bag, Edan's in it, shopping assistant and hide-and-seek champion! Edan is well supervised here, as you notice the handles are still on the bag. Tip: cut them off for safety

Treat Puzzle Alternatives:

- Toilet paper tubes with holes poked through (hide treats inside)
- Ice cube trays with treats in some compartments
- Muffin tins with treats hidden under tennis balls
- Paper bags with treats scattered inside (remove handles for safety).

CHAPTER 11
TRAINING & ENRICHMENT

The Cat Wheel Revolution

If you think a Bengal will be satisfied with just a few laps around the living room, think again. Enter the cat wheel, a giant hamster wheel for cats and the ultimate energy outlet for Bengals. When we first brought home the cat wheel, Edan looked at it suspiciously, then jumped on and immediately started running as if she were late for a meeting. Now, it's her favorite way to burn off steam, especially on rainy days.

Stormy: "When you need to hit your step count before breakfast."

Rotating Enrichment: Maintaining Novelty

The Weekly Rotation System:

- Monday: New cardboard configuration or hideout
- Wednesday: Different treat puzzle or food challenge
- Friday: Rearrange climbing furniture or add new perches
- Weekend: Special activities like supervised outdoor time or new toys.

The key is to change things before your Bengal gets bored, not after they start creating their own entertainment.

Understanding Scratching: Natural Behaviors

Scratching: Essential Bengal Maintenance

Why Scratching Isn't a Problem to Solve: Scratching serves multiple essential functions:

- Claw maintenance and shedding old sheaths
- Muscle stretching and exercise
- Scent marking and territory communication
- Stress relief and emotional regulation.

CHAPTER 11
TRAINING & ENRICHMENT

Directing Scratching Energy Appropriately

What Works in Our House:

- Multiple scratching surfaces in different textures (sisal, carpet, cardboard)
- Strategic placement near sleeping areas and room entrances
- Immediate replacement when scratching posts become worn
- Rewarding appropriate scratching with attention and treats.

Stormy vs. The New Furniture: A Lesson in Bengal Territorial Management

Whenever I bring home a new piece of furniture, Stormy is inevitably the first to investigate. Without fail, he'll approach the new arrival with the confidence of a quality inspector, conduct a thorough sniff examination, and then proceed to scratch it as if testing its worthiness for our home.

I've learned to anticipate this behavior and now place a new scratching post immediately next to any new furniture before Stormy even notices the arrival. This gives him an appropriate target for his territorial marking instincts, and he quickly shifts his attention to the designated scratcher instead of the expensive new sofa.

What this taught me about Bengal psychology: they aren't being destructive; they're expanding their territorial map by integrating new items. Providing a suitable scratching option right next to the tempting new furniture aligns with their natural instincts rather than opposing them. Bengals are quick learners when given the right choices, and Stormy consistently goes for the scratcher over the furniture when both are available.

Managing Excessive Vocalization

Understanding Bengal Communication Needs

Bengal cats yowling at 3 AM usually signal specific needs: boredom, hunger, a desire for attention, or sometimes just the joy of hearing their own voice echo through quiet houses.

Strategies That Reduce Nighttime Concerts:

- Vigorous evening play sessions to burn excess energy
- Puzzle feeders or hidden treats for nighttime entertainment
- Consistent bedtime routines that signal quiet time
- Ignoring attention-seeking vocalizations (harder than it sounds).

Chapter 11
Training & Enrichment

Edan's Night Routine: Edan loves a good "opera" at 2 a.m. If I give her a big play session before bed, she's much more likely to curl up quietly instead of serenading the moon.

If excessive vocalization develops suddenly, rule out medical issues before assuming it's behavioral. Pain, illness, or sensory changes can trigger increased vocalization.

Bengals on Patrol: Supervised Outdoor Adventures

Living on acres in the country, you'd think my Bengals, Edan and Stormy, would be off chasing kangaroos by now. But these two are strictly supervised explorers; think of them as tiny, stripy sheepdogs with a penchant for tree climbing and chicken diplomacy.

Before we head out, I attach their Tractive GPS trackers. Not only does Tractive show me exactly where my furry adventurers are at all times (and how far they've sprinted, stalked, or zigzagged), but it also provides a health report, so I can tell if Stormy's "zoomies" are Olympic-level or just everyday Bengal mischief. If I ever take my eyes off them, I have peace of mind knowing I can check the app and see their exact location; no Bengal left behind!

When I first open the door, they immediately race toward the large eucalyptus tree. They bolt so quickly you'd think they were about to hit the trunk, but at the last second, they're straight up, climbing as high as their wild heart's desire. This is exactly why I don't trim their claws: Bengals need those built-in crampons for safe tree descents (and dramatic entrances).

Edan and Stormy's idea of a walk? Straight up the nearest tree, because why take the path when you can take the vertical express!

Chapter 11
Training & Enrichment

GPS tracking is advised for all outdoor adventures. Keep visual contact and ensure recall training is in place before permitting supervised exploration.

Edan and Stormy are as loyal as dogs, trotting alongside me as we feed the alpacas (who, by the way, were raised with the cats and act as their unofficial bodyguards) and clean the chicken pen. The chickens and Bengals share a mutual admiration society; sometimes I wonder if the chickens think they're honorary Bengals, or vice versa.

Best of all, both Edan and Stormy are so well-trained that they come running when I call their names, usually from somewhere up a tree, covered in leaves, and looking very pleased with themselves.

Safe Outdoor Options for All Situations

For Supervised Outdoor Time:

- GPS tracking devices for peace of mind during exploration
- Secure, fenced areas where Bengals can climb and explore safely
- Always maintain visual contact - Bengal curiosity stops for no one

For Urban or Apartment Living:

- Harness and leash walks in quiet, secure areas
- Catios and enclosures for fresh air and sunshine
- Window boxes or mesh balconies for apartment dwellers
- Pet strollers for Bengals who want sights and smells without walking stress

Pro tip: If you want your Bengals to enjoy the great outdoors, always supervise them, use a GPS tracker like Tractive, and let them keep their claws for those high-speed eucalyptus climbs. Your cat, your wildlife, and your peace of mind will thank you.

Setting Realistic Training Expectations

Setting Realistic Expectations

What Training Can Achieve:

- Better communication between you and your Bengal
- Mental stimulation that reduces destructive behaviors
- Stronger bonds through positive interactions
- Practical skills like coming when called or using carriers willingly.

What Training Cannot Do:

- Eliminate all Bengal mischief (nor should it)
- Make your Bengal behave exactly like other cats
- Replace the need for adequate physical exercise and environmental enrichment.

Training and Enrichment Activities

Bengal Training Progress & Behavior Tracker

How to Use Your Tracker:

- Date: When the session happened or when you noticed a behavior
- Behavior/Skill: What you're targeting, think *"Come When Called"* or *"No Attacking Toes at 3 am"*
- Training Method: Treats, clicker, chin-chats, or good old patience
- Progress Notes: Triumphs, disasters, and *"curiosity got the cat again"* giggles
- Next Steps: What to repeat, change, or try next.

Access this tracker (and more goodies) as a printable from your free resource collection (see page 2). No typing required, just print and paw-scribe!

Training Progress & Behavior Tracker				
Date	Behavior/Skill	Training Method	Progress Notes	Next Steps

Make extra copies for new skills, weekly targets, or for each wild Bengal in your home!

Activity Ideas

Enrichment Bingo: Create a bingo card with activities like box play, puzzle feeder, fetch, and water play. Mark each activity off as your Bengal tries them; reward both of you when you fill a row!

Adventure Log: Record your Bengal's first harness walk, favorite outdoor sights, and any new skills learned. Note which environments make your Bengal most confident or curious.

Training Journal:

- Which behaviors is your Bengal learning easily vs. struggling with?
- What treats or rewards motivate them most effectively?
- When during the day are they most receptive to training?
- Are training sessions strengthening your relationship or creating stress?

Chapter 11
Training & Enrichment

Edan's Perspective:

"Training sessions are opportunities to demonstrate my intellectual superiority while earning treats for my cooperation. I learn quickly because I'm brilliant, not because I want to please humans. Keep the challenges interesting, the rewards substantial, and the sessions brief. I have important napping to schedule."

Stormy's Perspective:

"I approach training as a collaborative problem-solving exercise. Show me what you want, make it worth my while, and I'll participate enthusiastically. Rush the process or use boring rewards, and I'll find more interesting activities that don't require your supervision."

CHAPTER 11
TRAINING & ENRICHMENT

Final Thoughts

Training and enrichment for Bengals isn't about making perfectly obedient cats; it's about giving them suitable outlets for their intelligence, energy, and natural instincts. When you engage their minds and respect their individual personalities, training becomes a partnership that enhances your bond while keeping everyone happier. My experience with Edan and Stormy shows that the best training occurs when you're truly interested in what your Bengal finds engaging, rather than trying to force your agenda on their natural behaviors.

The goal is to create an environment where Bengal cats' intelligence can thrive safely and positively. Some days involve clicker training sessions; other days focus on appreciating their creative problem-solving, even when it means redesigning your carefully organized spaces.

Training and enrichment are about more than just keeping your Bengal out of trouble; they help create a bond filled with laughter, discovery, and mutual respect. Every clicker session, puzzle toy, or new scratching post is an opportunity to celebrate your Bengal's intelligence and spirit. Remember that every Bengal is unique in its learning style, motivation, and interests. What works brilliantly for one cat might completely fail with another. Stay flexible, keep your sense of humor, and celebrate the small victories along the way. When you combine structure, fun, and love, you and your Bengal will thrive together, mastering tricks, zoomies, and cardboard boxes as a team.

PART IV: FAMILY LIFE & ADVANCED TOPICS

Chapter 12
Socialization, Multi-Pet Homes

Bengals are social butterflies with wild streaks; they thrive on interaction, but their boldness and energy can make introductions with other pets or children feel like orchestrating a diplomatic summit. The key to success is understanding that Bengals approach new relationships with curiosity and confidence, but they need time and structure to build positive associations.

What I've learned from managing Edan and Stormy's social experiences: each introduction is unique, and patience, along with realistic expectations, leads to the best results.

Understanding Bengal Social Dynamics

The Confidence Factor

Bengals usually approach new situations with curiosity rather than fear. When my friend brought her daughter, Olivia, to visit, Edan immediately took on the role of the official greeting committee, thoroughly inspecting everything before settling in to supervise the entire playdate from her favorite perch.

What This Means for Introductions:

- Bengals often initiate contact rather than waiting passively
- Their confidence can be overwhelming for more timid animals
- They're usually more curious than aggressive, but supervision is always essential
- Early positive experiences shape their social expectations

Step-by-Step Pet Introductions

The Foundation: Scent Swapping

Before any face-to-face meetings, allow animals to familiarize themselves with each other's scents through careful exchanges.

What Works in Practice:

- Rub a clean cloth on each animal and place it near the other's food bowl
- Swap bedding between animals for several days
- Let the new pet explore Bengal territory when Bengals are in another room
- Use baby gates for visual contact without physical interaction

Timeline That Works: Plan on 1-2 weeks of scent introduction before attempting visual contact, longer if either animal shows stress signs.

Visual Introductions: The Careful Reveal

Our Approach to New Situations:

- Begin with cracked doors or baby gates that allow limited visual contact
- Keep sessions short (5-10 minutes) and always end on a positive note
- Have treats ready to create positive associations
- Watch body language carefully, relaxed postures vs. tension or aggression

Remember: you're looking for calm curiosity, not immediate friendship. Tolerance is initially a perfectly successful outcome.

Bengal and Dog Dynamics: The Reality from My Experience

When Dogs Visit Our House

Edan and Stormy have shown me that not all Bengals are the social butterflies you read about online. When friends bring their dogs over, both cats strategically retreat to the bedroom to avoid the canine invasion.

What I've Observed:

- Immediate hiding when dogs arrive (not fear, just territorial management)
- Staying concealed for the entire visit, regardless of the dog's behavior
- No interest in gradual introductions or *"getting used to"* visiting dogs
- Quick return to normal behavior once dogs leave.

Signs This Approach Works for Them:

- No stress behaviors like overgrooming or litter box avoidance
- Normal appetite and activity levels after visits
- Confident territorial behavior in their own spaces
- Calm observation from secure vantage points

This taught me that not every Bengal needs to be social with all kinds of animals. Sometimes, the best relationship is respectful avoidance.

For Permanent Dog Additions

Important Limitation: My experience only involves visiting dogs, not permanently integrating them into households. If you plan to add a dog to your Bengal home, research resources specifically about permanent cat-dog introductions and consider consulting animal behaviorists for guidance.

Chapter 12
Socialization, Multi-Pet Homes

What I Can Share from Observation:

- Bengals need secure retreat spaces during any dog interactions
- High perches and escape routes are essential for cat confidence
- Supervised, gradual introductions work better than "throwing them together"
- Individual personalities matter more than breed generalizations.

Testimonial from a Bengal Parent:

Introducing Hunter (our Bengal boy) to our dog, Max, was like watching a comedy sketch. Hunter approached with a confident chirp, Max wagged his tail in confusion, and within minutes, they were chasing each other around the living room, partners in mischief from day one. Bengals have a knack for turning strangers into friends and for making every introduction a story worth retelling.

"Bengal rule #12: Make friends with the dog and you'll always have the best seat in the house! Early socialization means more snuggles (and strategic perching) for everyone."

Activity: Introduction Journal

- Keep a daily log of each pet's reactions, stress signals, and which treats worked best.
- Note small improvements, like a shared sniff or a relaxed tail, and celebrate progress.

CHAPTER 12
SOCIALIZATION, MULTI-PET HOMES

Multi-Cat Households: Managing Bengal Personalities

Life with Two Bengals: What Actually Happened

When Stormy joined our household six months after Edan, I watched them negotiate territorial agreements with fascinating diplomacy. There was no dramatic confrontation; instead, they developed a resource-sharing system that still governs their relationship.

Stormy knows comfort; once he's claimed the chair, everyone else must wait their turn!

"Their resource-sharing system operates like a tiny United Nations with fuzzy ambassadors. Treaty negotiations over the sunny windowsill happen through strategic positioning, slow blinks, and occasionally, Stormy's signature move of simply flopping down wherever Edan was planning to sit."

Their Natural Settlement:

- Stormy immediately claimed the chair with the plush blanket; Edan kept her windowsill kingdom
- Different feeding stations prevented competition
- Separate litter box preferences emerged naturally (Edan: study, Stormy: laundry room)
- Morning vs. evening lap time scheduling was developed without human intervention.

What Made Multi-Bengal Life Work

Practical Strategies:

- Multiple everything: litter boxes, feeding stations, sleeping spots, climbing trees
- Vertical territory expansion so both cats could claim high spaces
- Respecting their individual preferences rather than forcing interactions
- Separate attention time when one cat clearly wanted solo human interaction.

CHAPTER 12
SOCIALIZATION, MULTI-PET HOMES

Signs of Successful Cohabitation:

- Sleeping near (but not necessarily with) each other
- No resource guarding around food or favorite humans
- Occasional mutual grooming sessions (rare but precious)
- Playing separately without hiding from each other

"What surprised me: these two became inseparable best friends who are practically joined at the hip. They play together, sleep in adorable cuddle puddles, and their only 'fights' involve Stormy's terrible timing when he decides it's party time while Edan is mid-beauty sleep. Watching Stormy try to coax a sleepy Edan into playing is like watching someone try to wake a teenager on a Saturday morning, lots of gentle pawing, strategic placement of toys, and eventually just lying down next to her with dramatic sighs until she surrenders to his enthusiasm."

Bengal-Children Interactions: Supervised Success Stories

The Olivia Visit: A Case Study

When my friend and her daughter, Olivia, visited for the weekend, I was curious (and a bit nervous) to see how Edan and Stormy would handle a small human in their territory. Edan, always curious, sat at the edge of the action, eyes wide and whiskers twitching as if doing a thorough inspection. Within minutes, she hopped down, circled our guest, and settled in with a look that clearly said, *"You may proceed, but I'll be supervising."*

Stormy, meanwhile, watched from a safe distance, tail flicking with interest. Once he saw Edan getting gentle head scratches and a giggle or two, his confidence grew. Before long, both cats were *"helping"* with the block tower, Edan batting stray pieces, and Stormy sprawling across the play mat as if to claim it for Team Bengal.

CHAPTER 12
SOCIALIZATION, MULTI-PET HOMES

What Made It Work:

- Clear rules for the child: gentle hands, no grabbing tails, no sudden movements
- Supervised interactions with immediate intervention if needed
- Teaching the child how to let Edan approach rather than pursuing her
- Respect for Edan's retreat signals when she needed space

The Breakthrough Moment: When Olivia offered Edan a toy mouse, Edan gently accepted it, dropped it at the child's feet, and patiently waited for a game of fetch. This demonstrated both her trust and her natural tendency to include interested humans in her activities.

Child-Proofing Bengal Relationships

Essential Safety Rules:

- Always supervise interactions between children and Bengals
- Teach children to read cat body language and respect boundaries
- Provide escape routes so cats never feel cornered
- Establish quiet spaces where cats can retreat from child activity

What Children Need to Learn:

- How to pet gently along a cat's back (never against the fur)
- Recognition of *"I need space"* signals (flattened ears, twitching tail)
- Appropriate play activities using toys rather than hands
- When to give cats alone time vs. when interaction is welcomed.

When Introductions Don't Go According to Plan

Recognizing When to Step Back

Warning Signs from My Experience:

- Prolonged hiding that extends beyond regular adjustment periods
- Resource guarding behaviors around food, litter boxes, or favorite humans
- Stress-related changes in eating, grooming, or elimination habits
- Escalating tension rather than gradual acceptance

Problem-Solving Strategies

What Worked When Edan Initially Guarded Resources:

- Returned to complete separation and a slower reintroduction process
- Added more resources (additional litter boxes, feeding stations)
- Increased individual attention time to reduce competition feelings
- Extended the timeline rather than rushing toward cohabitation

When to Seek Professional Help:

- Aggression that escalates despite careful management
- Persistent stress behaviors in any animal are involved
- Resource competition that doesn't improve with environmental changes
- Your own stress levels are becoming unmanageable

Sometimes the kindest approach is recognizing that some animals aren't suited for permanent cohabitation, regardless of careful introduction techniques.

Activity: Bengal & Kids Checklist

- Did everyone use gentle hands?
- Was playtime supervised?
- Did your Bengal have a safe retreat?
- Did you reward positive interactions?

Light-Hearted Bengal Truth:

Remember, even the most carefully planned plans can go awry when a Bengal is involved. Sometimes you'll feel like a zookeeper, other times like a referee, and sometimes like the audience at the funniest show in town. Celebrate small wins and laugh at the chaos; your Bengal will too.

Activity: Socialization Progress Tracker

- Create a table for each pet and note daily interactions, stress signals, and joyous moments.
- Use stickers or colored pens for each successful step.
- Share your progress with family or in Bengal owner groups for support.

Edan's giving Storm the classic 'new roommate' inspection, just making sure he knows who's boss of the cat tree!

CHAPTER 12
SOCIALIZATION, MULTI-PET HOMES

Success Stories: Unexpected Friendships

Edan and Ruby the Turtle

One of our most unexpected household relationships developed between Edan and Ruby, our turtle. Edan makes daily visits to Ruby's habitat, sometimes dabbing a paw in the water for a gentle *"hello,"* while Ruby seems to enjoy following the cats around during her supervised exploration time.

Edan, mid-leap, checking in on her aquatic sister Ruby. "Don't worry, I'm just here for a quick chat and maybe a paw dip!

It's proof that Bengals' social nature extends beyond typical cat-dog-human relationships.

Whether your Bengal befriends the family dog, tolerates the neighbor's visiting parrot, or develops an unusual bond with a completely different species, their curious and adaptable nature often leads to unexpected relationships. The key is always supervising these interactions and ensuring safety for all animals involved.

Safety Considerations:

- Never leave different species unsupervised together
- Ensure all animals have secure retreat spaces
- Monitor stress levels in all pets during any interactions
- Maintain appropriate hygiene between different animal habitats.

CHAPTER 12
SOCIALIZATION, MULTI-PET HOMES

In every household with Bengals and turtles, expect a cross-species standoff worthy of a nature documentary (with more fur and giggles). Remember, a Bengal's expression is worth a thousand words and often at least twice as many laughs.

Edan and Ruby: proof that in Bengal's world, friendship knows no boundaries or species!

Activity: Socialization Progress Assessment

Weekly Relationship Monitoring

Questions to Evaluate:

- Are all pets eating, sleeping, and using facilities usually?
- What positive interactions have you observed this week?
- Are there any signs of stress or territorial disputes?
- Which environmental modifications seem to be helping most?

Monthly Social Dynamic Review:

- How have relationships evolved since initial introductions?
- Are current arrangements working for all family members (human and animal)?
- What adjustments might improve harmony or reduce stress?
- Do any situations require professional consultation?

Chapter 12
Socialization, Multi-Pet Homes

Edan's Perspective:

"I approach new household members with appropriate caution and thorough evaluation. Some creatures earn my approval through respectful behavior and interesting activities. Others are tolerated from a distance. Children who bring toys and understand proper petting techniques receive higher approval ratings than those who grab tails."

Stormy's Perspective:

"Every new family member deserves a fair assessment period. I prefer gradual introductions with plenty of escape routes and minimal pressure for immediate friendship. Dogs are loud and unpredictable, but children who sit quietly and let me approach often become acceptable companions."

Final Thoughts

Successful socialization with Bengals depends on respecting their unique personalities while offering structured opportunities for positive interactions. Not every Bengal will enjoy every type of companion, and that's perfectly normal.

What I've learned from various social experiments is that the best relationships form when you focus on creating positive associations instead of forcing interactions. Bengals are naturally curious, but they need to feel secure and in control of their social experiences.

The key is patience, realistic expectations, and genuine respect for what each animal communicates about their comfort levels. Some Bengals become social ambassadors who welcome everyone; others prefer selective relationships with carefully chosen companions. Both approaches can lead to harmonious households when managed thoughtfully.

Remember that every introduction is unique, influenced by individual personalities, past experiences, and current stress levels. Stay observant, remain flexible, and celebrate small victories along the way. The goal isn't perfect friendship; it's peaceful coexistence that helps everyone feel secure and content in their shared space.

Chapter 13
Routines for Lifelong Happiness

I wake up each morning to find Stormy stretched out beside me full length and Edan curled on the other side, purring softly. Sometimes Stormy sits at the window watching the sunrise, both eagerly waiting for their breakfast. This isn't an accident, it's the result of two years of gentle routine-building that turned chaotic Bengal energy into predictable, comforting rhythms.

Our daily routines, morning coffee cuddles, evening play sessions, and quiet weekend moments have become the heart of our home. With the Bengals, each day brings new adventures, but the steady rhythm of routine keeps those adventures joyful instead of overwhelming.

Why Bengals Need Routines More Than Other Cats

Bengals are wired differently. Their wild ancestry gives them intelligence that craves patterns and energy that needs outlets. Without structure, that intelligence turns into mischief, and that energy becomes destructive chaos. I learned this the hard way during Edan's first week, when she treated my house like an all-you-can-explore buffet, leaving a trail of toppled plants and opened drawers in her wake.

Routines give Bengals what their leopard cat ancestors had in the wild: predictable hunting times, safe resting spots, and territorial boundaries. In our homes, breakfast becomes the morning hunt, play sessions replace prey capture, and designated napping spots provide security.

Edan, Dad, and the Fire-Lighting Antics

One of Edan's proudest moments was *"helping"* Dad light the fireplace. As soon as the firewood was bought out, Edan was there, sniffing, batting at kindling, and finally sitting squarely in front of the hearth as if she'd personally invented fire. Dad's attempts to build a tidy stack were interrupted by a Bengal paw swiping sticks in all directions. In the end, Edan supervised from a safe distance, looking very pleased with her contribution to family warmth.

CHAPTER 13
ROUTINES FOR LIFELONG HAPPINESS

Edan, ever the supervisor, helped Dad light the fire. Bengals love to be part of every family ritual, even if it's just to check your technique!

What Routines Do for Bengal Families:

For Your Bengal:

- Reduces anxiety by creating predictable patterns
- Channels energy into appropriate outlets
- Builds security through consistent expectations
- Provides mental stimulation through anticipated activities

For You:

- Prevents destructive behaviors through proactive management
- Creates bonding opportunities at predictable times
- Reduces stress by knowing what to expect when
- Builds a framework for managing two high-energy cats

The difference I noticed was transformative. Before establishing routines, I was constantly reacting, cleaning up messes, redirecting energy, and managing chaos. After routines took hold, I became proactive, anticipating needs, channeling energy positively, and actually enjoying the lively Bengal personality instead of feeling overwhelmed by it.

Chapter 13
Routines for Lifelong Happiness

The Magic of Morning Rituals

Morning coffee is never lonely in our house; Edan and Stormy curl up on my lap while I read my Kindle, turning every breakfast into a cozy, purring ritual. This didn't happen overnight; it took months of patient training. Not training them, mind you, but training myself to sit still long enough for two cats to settle into the perfect lap formation. Apparently, there's a very specific protocol for optimal Bengal distribution that I was previously unaware of.

The key was making myself available at the same time every morning. Bengals are creatures of habit, and once they realized 6:30 AM meant *"human lap time,"* they started anticipating and getting ready for it. Edan now waits by the coffee maker, while Stormy stretches comfortably on the couch, saving my spot.

Morning coffee is never lonely in our house; Edan and Stormy curl up on my lap while I read my Kindle, turning every breakfast into a purring, cozy ritual

Building Your Morning Routine:

- Choose a realistic wake-up time and stick to it (weekends included initially)
- Start with 10-15 minutes of quiet interaction before the day's chaos
- Include physical contact, lap time, gentle brushing, or chin scratches
- Keep it simple and repeatable, even on rushed mornings

CHAPTER 13
ROUTINES FOR LIFELONG HAPPINESS

Daily Structure That Works

Here's the routine that transformed our household from Bengal bedlam to harmonious rhythm:

MORNING ROUTINE (6:30-8:00 AM):

- Coffee and lap time (20 minutes)
- High-energy play session with wand toys (15 minutes)
- Fresh breakfast with puzzle feeders
- Window watching while I get ready for work

MIDDAY STRUCTURE (11:00 AM-2:00 PM):

- Rotating solo toys (puzzle balls, catnip mice)
- Second meal in treat-dispensing toys
- Designated nap time in sunny spots
- Background nature videos for entertainment

EVENING WIND-DOWN (6:00-9:00 PM):

- Intense play session to burn remaining energy (20-30 minutes)
- Dinner followed by grooming time
- Family interaction, TV watching, and reading together
- Quiet activities like gentle brushing or slow puzzle games

The evening routine is just as important as the morning one. Bengals need assistance transitioning from *"day mode"* to *"sleep mode,"* and consistent evening activities indicate that it's time to settle down.

Weekend and Flexible Scheduling

Weekends don't mean abandoning routines; they mean adapting them. Saturday mornings might feature longer play sessions or special breakfast treats, but the core structure stays the same. This provides you with flexibility while still offering the security your Bengal craves.

Weekend Variations:

- Extend morning cuddle time to 30-45 minutes
- Add special activities like supervised outdoor time or new puzzle toys
- Include grooming sessions or nail trims in the routine
- Maintain meal times even if play times shift.

"Weekend lie-ins are a negotiation. Edan believes 6:30 AM is 6:30 AM regardless of work schedules, while Stormy is willing to accept a 15-minute grace period for extended cuddle privileges. Compromise is possible, but it involves significant treat-based diplomacy."

For Busy Days:

- Prepare puzzle feeders the night before
- Use automatic toys or TV programming for midday entertainment
- Focus on quality over quantity in shortened play sessions
- Never skip morning or evening interaction entirely

When Routines Get Disrupted

Life happens. Travel, schedule changes, visitors, or illness can disrupt carefully crafted routines. The importance lies in planning for interruptions and preparing recovery strategies.

"Travel preparation involves creating detailed instructions that read like a diplomatic treaty: 'Stormy requires exactly 4.5 minutes of chin scratches before breakfast; Edan expects her morning sun patch to be properly warmed by 6:45 AM; and both cats will conduct a formal inspection of any sitter's qualifications through strategic leg weaving and treat-dispensing tests."

Travel Preparation:

- Gradually adjust routine timing a week before leaving
- Arrange for sitters to maintain core elements (meal times, play sessions)
- Leave detailed routine instructions and emergency contacts
- Use familiar toys and blankets to maintain comfort

Schedule Changes:

- Shift routines gradually (15 minutes earlier/later each day)
- Maintain the sequence even if timing changes
- Use food motivation to help adjust to new schedules
- Be patient, it takes 2-3 weeks to fully establish new patterns

Seasonal Adjustments: Winter routines might include more indoor enrichment and heat sources, while summer schedules could shift to cooler morning playtimes. The key is maintaining the pattern while adapting to environmental changes.

"Summer routines shift to cooler morning playtimes when Edan decides the afternoon sun is too undignified for athletic activities. Winter schedules include strategic heating pad negotiations and extended indoor enrichment sessions. Spring brings the Great Window Supervision Season, where both cats become full-time bird-watching consultants."

Chapter 13
Routines for Lifelong Happiness

Making Routines Work for Multi-Cat Households

With two Bengals, I learned that individual attention within group routines works best. Edan and Stormy have different energy levels and preferences, but they share the same schedule framework.

"Individual needs within shared routines require diplomatic scheduling. Edan prefers her morning play session to include dramatic leaping and curtain involvement, while Stormy favors ground-level tactical maneuvers and strategic treat positioning. The key is sequential rather than simultaneous activities; trying to manage both Bengal play styles at once is like conducting an orchestra where half the musicians are performing jazz and the other half are playing classical."

Time	Activity	Edan's Role	Stormy's Role
6:30 AM	Coffee & Lap Time	Chief Lap Inspector	Cushion Warmer
7:00 AM	Play Session	Athletic Director	Enthusiastic Participant
7:30 AM	Breakfast	Quality Control	Appreciative Consumer

Individual Needs Within Shared Routines:

- Separate feeding stations to prevent competition
- Rotating one-on-one play sessions alongside group activities
- Multiple napping spots to prevent territorial disputes, although Edan and Stormy love to nap together, and the change in locations.
- Individual grooming time for cats who prefer private attention

Troubleshooting Common Routine Challenges

"My Bengal treats schedule changes like a personal betrayal": This is completely normal Bengal drama. They've memorized your routine down to the minute and consider any deviation a breach of contract. Stormy once staged a one-cat protest when daylight saving time shifted breakfast by an

Chapter 13
Routines for Lifelong Happiness

hour, sitting pointedly by his empty bowl and giving me disappointed looks until I consulted the atomic clock.

"My Bengal won't settle into routines": Start smaller. Instead of implementing a full schedule, begin with just morning feeding time. Once that's consistent, add one element per week.

"Routines work during the week but fall apart on weekends": Weekend flexibility is fine, but maintain core elements like meal times and at least one play session. Think *"routine adaptation"* rather than *"routine abandonment."*

"My work schedule is too unpredictable": Focus on duration rather than specific times. Your Bengal needs 30 minutes of focused interaction daily, whether that's 6 AM or 9 PM, matters less than consistency once you choose.

"My Bengal gets destructive when routines change": This is normal! Increase environmental enrichment during transitions and provide extra attention. Some cats need a week to adjust to schedule changes.

DAILY BENGAL ROUTINE FRAMEWORK

The Long-Term Payoff

Two years into our routine, I can anticipate Edan and Stormy's needs, moods, and energy levels. They've learned to trust that playtime will happen, that food will be available, and that cuddles are part of every day. This mutual predictability has strengthened our bond significantly.

Routines aren't about rigidity; they're about creating a framework that allows Bengal personalities to flourish within boundaries that work for everyone. A well-planned routine isn't just about keeping your cat happy; it's about creating a lifestyle where Bengal energy enhances your life instead of exhausting it.

Activity: Creating Your Bengal Routine Chart

Create a weekly chart with columns for morning interaction, play sessions, meals, and evening wind-down:

- Mark off each activity daily for two weeks
- Note what your Bengal enjoys most and when they seem most active
- Adjust timing based on your observations
- Celebrate successful routine weeks with special treats or new toys

Chapter 13
Routines for Lifelong Happiness

Tip: Mix things up weekly by trying a new scent, rearranging climbing shelves, or organizing a scavenger hunt to keep your Bengal's mind stimulated.

Sample Bengal Routine Chart

Time	Activity	Notes
7:00 am	Play & breakfast	Wand toys, wet food
12:00 pm	Puzzle feeder/enrichment	Window perch time
6:00 pm	Clicker training & dinner	New toy/rotation
9:00 pm	Wind-down cuddles	Soft music

Activity: Bengal Routine Success Tracker

Week 1-2: Observation Phase

- Note natural activity peaks and rest periods
- Track meal preferences and timing
- Observe favorite cuddle times and play preferences

Week 3-4: Implementation Phase

- Establish consistent wake-up and meal times
- Introduce structured play sessions
- Create predictable wind-down routines

Month 2+: Refinement Phase

- Adjust timing based on what works
- Add seasonal variations
- Celebrate routine successes with special activities

"The real magic of Bengal routines isn't just about managing behavior; it's how predictable rhythms strengthen your bond. When Edan knows that evening cuddles are guaranteed, she can focus on more meaningful activities, like perfecting her dramatic entrances and overseeing household tasks. When Stormy trusts that morning lap time is sacred, he becomes more adventurous during the day, confident that his comfort time is secure."

Edan's Perspective:

"Routines aren't boring, they're royal scheduling. I know exactly when my subjects (that's you) will provide breakfast, entertainment, and proper worship. Predictability means I can focus on more important things, like perfecting my curtain-climbing technique and training you to respond to my various meows."

Stormy's Perspective:

"I like knowing what comes next. Morning snuggles, then breakfast, then window watching, it's comforting. When everything has its time and place, I can relax and enjoy being a Bengal instead of wondering what's happening next. Plus, routine cuddles are the best cuddles."

CHAPTER 13
ROUTINES FOR LIFELONG HAPPINESS

Final Thoughts

Building routines with Bengals is like learning to dance with a partner full of energy and strong opinions. It requires patience, consistency, and adaptability. But once you find your rhythm, every day becomes a celebration of the special joy that comes from sharing your life with these extraordinary cats.

Whether you're a busy professional, a family with kids, or a retiree, a Bengal's daily routine can improve your lifestyle with a little creativity and consistent effort. Start small, stay steady, and enjoy watching chaos turn into the comfortable predictability that makes every day with your Bengal an adventure worth looking forward to.

Remember: every day is a new opportunity to strengthen the bond that makes Bengals truly unforgettable companions.

Chapter 14
Senior Bengal Care

Preparing for the Journey Ahead

As Edan approaches five and Stormy turns four, I'm not writing this chapter from the perspective of caring for senior cats; I'm writing it as someone preparing for that journey. While both cats are still in their athletic prime, occasionally I catch glimpses of what might be early signs of maturity: Edan takes slightly longer stretches after her afternoon naps, and Stormy sometimes chooses the lower branch of his cat tree instead of the penthouse suite.

These aren't signs of aging problems; they're just natural shifts that remind me to pay attention and prepare for the senior years ahead. What I can share is the research I've done, the conversations I've had with other Bengal owners whose cats have gracefully aged, and the foundations I'm building now to ensure Edan and Stormy's golden years are comfortable and dignified.

This chapter reflects preparation and research rather than hands-on experience. Every Bengal ages differently, and I'll be learning alongside you as Edan and Stormy move through their senior years. What I can offer are the foundations I'm building now and the wisdom I've gathered from others who've walked this path.

CHAPTER 14
SENIOR BENGAL CARE

Understanding When "Senior" Actually Begins

Most cats are considered seniors around age 7 to 10, but Bengals often maintain their youthful energy well beyond these typical markers. From what other Bengal owners have told me, the transition tends to be gradual rather than dramatic, subtle changes in preferences and capabilities rather than sudden limitations.

Early Signs I'm Learning to Watch For

What experienced Bengal owners have shared:

- Slightly longer recovery times after intensive play sessions
- Preference for lower jumping routes to favorite perches
- More deliberate movements, especially first thing in the morning
- Increased appreciation for warm, soft resting spots
- Gradual changes in sleep patterns or preferred sleeping locations

What I'm observing now: Even at four and five, I'm starting to notice subtle changes. Edan occasionally stretches a bit longer after her morning nap, and Stormy sometimes takes the scenic route to his favorite windowsill instead of his usual dramatic leap. These observations aren't worrying; they're teaching me to pay attention to their individual patterns.

Research-Based Health Monitoring

What Veterinarians Recommend for Aging Bengals

Preventive Care Schedule:

- Biannual checkups starting around age 7
- Annual blood work to establish baseline values
- Regular dental assessments and cleaning
- Heart monitoring for HCM (particularly important for Bengals)
- Weight and body condition tracking

Early Detection Strategies:

- Monthly home health checks
- Documentation of appetite, drinking, and elimination patterns
- Mobility assessments during play and daily activities
- Behavioral change monitoring

I'm beginning these monitoring routines now while Edan and Stormy are healthy, so I'll have baseline patterns to compare as they age.

Environmental Modifications: Preparing Before You Need Them

What Other Bengal Owners Recommend

Based on conversations with owners of senior Bengals, here are modifications that become helpful:

Access Improvements:

- Ramps or steps to favorite perches (can be added gradually)
- Lower-sided litter boxes for easier entry and exit
- Raised food and water bowls to reduce neck strain
- Additional litter boxes on the main living level
- Orthopedic bedding in preferred resting spots

Comfort Enhancements:

- Heated beds or pet-safe heating pads
- Draft-free sleeping areas with easy escape routes
- Non-slip rugs on smooth floors for better traction
- Easy-access hideouts for quiet time

The key insight from experienced owners: implement changes gradually before they're urgently needed, so cats can adapt while they're still confident and mobile.

Nutritional Planning for the Future

What Research Suggests for Senior Bengal Nutrition

Dietary Considerations:

- Higher-quality, easily digestible proteins become more important
- Enhanced hydration support through wet food or water fountains
- Joint support supplements may benefit cats showing stiffness
- Smaller, more frequent meals often work better than large portions

Feeding Adaptations:

- Elevated food bowls to reduce neck strain
- Consistent meal times for security and routine
- High-quality senior-specific diets, when recommended by veterinarians
- Enhanced palatability for cats who become pickier eaters

I'm already establishing feeding routines and preferences that will adapt well to senior needs.

Building Senior-Friendly Routines Now

Creating Adaptable Daily Patterns

What I'm Implementing Early:

- Consistent meal and interaction times that can be maintained regardless of mobility changes
- Multiple comfortable resting options throughout the house
- Gentle daily handling to maintain acceptance of health monitoring
- Flexible play sessions that can be adjusted for changing energy levels.

Routine Elements That Age Well:

- Predictable quiet times for extended rest
- Multiple short interaction sessions rather than long, intensive ones
- Comfortable social time without pressure for athletic performance
- Gradual transitions between activities.

Preparing for Common Senior Health Issues

Bengal-Specific Aging Considerations

What Veterinarians and Breeders Warn About:

- Hypertrophic Cardiomyopathy (HCM): May not show symptoms until advanced
- Arthritis: Can affect climbing and jumping abilities
- Kidney function changes: Common in all aging cats
- Dental disease: Impacts overall health and comfort
- Vision or hearing changes: May require environmental adaptations.

Early Intervention Strategies:

- Establishing baseline health values while cats are young
- Building relationships with veterinarians experienced in senior cat care
- Creating an emergency fund specifically for age-related health needs
- Learning to recognize subtle signs of discomfort or illness.

Quality of Life Preparation

Learning to Assess Senior Cat Wellbeing

Monthly Questions I'm Learning to Ask:

- Are they able to access their favorite resting spots comfortably?
- Do they maintain interest in food, social interaction, and basic activities?
- Can they use the litter box without apparent discomfort?
- Do they seek out enjoyable activities like window watching or gentle play?
- Are they experiencing more good days than difficult ones?

When Professional Support Becomes Important

Resources to Establish Early:

- Veterinarians experienced with senior cat care
- Understanding of pain management options
- Feline behaviorists for age-related behavioral changes
- Alternative therapy options (where available)

Financial Planning for Senior Care

What Experienced Owners Wish They'd Known

Budget Considerations:

- Senior health monitoring costs increase
- Potential need for specialized diets or medications
- Environmental modification expenses
- Emergency medical fund for age-related conditions

Insurance Considerations:

- Starting coverage early, before age-related conditions develop
- Understanding policy limitations for senior care
- Evaluating coverage for breed-specific health issues

I'm building this financial foundation now, while veterinary costs are routine rather than critical.

Creating Memories and Traditions

What I'm Doing Now to Prepare

Documentation:

- Regular photos and videos of their current athletic abilities
- Recording their favorite activities and preferences
- Noting their unique personality quirks and behaviors
- Creating a health and preference history for future caregivers

Relationship Building:

- Deepening bonds through consistent daily interactions
- Teaching them to accept gentle handling and health checks
- Building positive associations with carriers and veterinary visits
- Creating comfort routines that they can rely on throughout their lives.

Activity: Senior Care Preparation Checklist

What to Establish While Cats Are Young

Health Monitoring Foundation:

- Monthly weight checks and body condition assessment
- Baseline behavior and activity pattern documentation
- Veterinary relationship establishment
- Emergency care plan development

Environmental Assessment:

- Identify potential mobility challenges in the current setup
- Plan future modification locations and timing
- Establish comfort zones that can be enhanced later
- Create multiple access routes to essential areas

Financial Preparation:

- Senior care savings fund establishment
- Insurance evaluation and selection
- Emergency expense planning
- Healthcare provider research

Chapter 14
Senior Bengal Care

Senior Bengal Wellness: Quick Reference Table

Wellness Area	Owner Actions
Vet Care	Check-ups every 6 months; routine labwork
Diet & Hydration	Senior-formulated food; fresh water; monitor portions
Dental Health	Tooth brushing; annual dental exam
Mobility & Joints	Ramps; joint supplements; accessible amenities
Comfort	Warm, draft-free beds nearby; easy access everywhere
Grooming	Gentle brushing a few times each week
Monitoring	Watch for appetite, weight, and personality changes
Enrichment	Short, interactive playtimes; food puzzles

Wisdom from the Bengal Community

What Long-Time Bengal Owners Share

Common Themes:

- "Start monitoring routines early, you'll be grateful for the baseline data"
- "Small environmental changes made gradually are accepted better than major modifications"
- "Senior Bengals still have strong personalities, respect their preferences"
- "Quality of life matters more than quantity, focus on comfort and dignity"

Practical Advice:

- "Take videos of their athletic prime, you'll treasure them later"
- "Build relationships with senior-focused veterinarians before you need them"
- "Don't rush to 'help' unless they're actually struggling; independence matters"
- "Every day is precious, but senior days can be especially sweet"

Bengals mellow with age, but their spark is forever. Senior Bengals still love a zoomie, though it may be a dignified, one-room dash. Treasure that wild spirit!

Chapter 14
Senior Bengal Care

Edan's Perspective:

"While I'm nowhere near ready for retirement from my athletic career, I appreciate that my humans are planning for my royal senior years. I expect the same high standards of service, with additional comfort accommodations and possibly more frequent treat distributions. Quality of life should never decline, only adapt to include more luxurious napping arrangements."

Stormy's Perspective:

"I'm still in my prime cuddle years, but I like knowing that future comfort is being planned. As long as lap time remains sacred and my favorite sunny spots stay available, I'm confident we can adapt to whatever changes come. Plus, senior status might come with additional treats, which sounds promising."

Final Thoughts

Preparing for senior Bengal care while your cats are still young isn't about anticipating problems; it's about building foundations that will serve you well throughout your journey together. The monitoring routines, environmental awareness, and relationship building you establish now will make future transitions smoother and less stressful for everyone involved.

What strikes me most about preparing for this phase is how it deepens my appreciation for Edan and Stormy's current vitality. Knowing that their athletic prime won't last forever makes every dramatic leap, every midnight zoomie session, and every perfect cat tree landing more precious.

The goal isn't to extend life at any cost, but to ensure that whatever time we have together is lived with comfort, dignity, and joy. Senior Bengals still have preferences, personalities, and the capacity for happiness; they need thoughtful support to express these fully.

Every day with a Bengal is a gift, whether they're young athletes or dignified seniors. By preparing now, we're ensuring that the gift keeps giving throughout all the phases of their remarkable lives.

Ask me again in five years, and I'll have stories to add to this research. For now, we're all learning and preparing together, building the foundation for whatever adventures lie ahead.

Chapter 14
Senior Bengal Care

Note: This chapter will evolve as Edan and Stormy age, adding real experience to complement the preparation and research presented here. The journey continues, and future editions will reflect the wisdom gained through actual senior Bengal care.

"As you plan for your Bengal's future, having the right products and resources becomes increasingly important. From the kitten supplies you'll need immediately to the specialized items that might benefit senior cats later, knowing where to find quality Bengal-appropriate products can make every stage of ownership smoother."

Chapter 15
Resources and Shopping Guide

After two years of trial, error, and sometimes costly mistakes with Edan and Stormy, I've realized that Bengal shopping is less about finding the "perfect" products and more about understanding which features truly matter for cats that treat your house like their personal gym. Fancy toys often lose out to cardboard boxes, expensive beds are ignored in favor of your clean laundry, and the so-called "indestructible" items eventually meet their match in determined Bengal engineering skills.

Edan once conducted a three-hour structural integrity assessment of a $200 cat tree, only to reject it in favor of the cardboard box it arrived in. The box became her fortress for six months; the tree became an expensive coat rack. This taught me that Bengal quality standards operate on a completely different economic system than human logic.

What this chapter offers: starting points for your own research, important selection criteria, and lessons learned from our household's product testing department (Edan and Stormy take their quality control responsibilities very seriously).

CHAPTER 15
RESOURCES AND SHOPPING GUIDE

The Reality of Bengal Product Reviews

How Edan and Stormy Evaluate New Purchases

Edan's Testing Protocol:

1. Thorough sniff inspection for acceptable scent levels
2. Structural integrity assessment (can this be climbed, knocked over, or relocated?)
3. Entertainment value evaluation (does this provide adequate mental stimulation?)
4. Comfort rating (suitable for royal napping standards?)
5. Final approval based on treat-dispensing potential

Stormy's Quality Control Process:

1. Patient observation from a safe distance
2. Cautious initial contact with one paw
3. Gradual full-body investigation if the item passes preliminary tests
4. Comfort assessment through extended testing periods
5. Long-term approval based on consistent performance and coziness factor

Their reviews don't always match manufacturer claims or online ratings. Bengal standards are unique and highly personal, based on quality metrics that no human focus group could predict.

Shopping with Bengal consultants means accepting that your carefully researched purchase list will be thoroughly audited by creatures who consider Amazon delivery day a personal holiday. Every box is inspected, every bag is investigated, and every new item receives a formal assessment that would put professional product testers to shame.

Essential Shopping Categories: What Actually Matters

Litter Boxes: The Archaeological Expedition

I thought I understood cat bathroom habits until I witnessed Stormy's first litter box session. What I expected to be a quick, tidy affair turned into what I can only describe as an archaeological excavation. Stormy approached the standard-sized box I'd purchased and began digging with the enthusiasm of someone searching for buried treasure.

Within minutes, litter was flying in a three-foot radius around the box. Stormy continued his excavation project, completely focused on creating what appeared to be the perfect bathroom environment according to very specific Bengal engineering standards. When he finally settled down to business, half the litter was decorating my laundry room floor.

Chapter 15
Resources and Shopping Guide

That weekend, I invested in high-sided boxes that could contain Stormy's construction projects. The difference was immediate; his digging satisfaction remained high, but the litter stayed where it belonged. Edan, meanwhile, gave the new boxes her royal approval with a dignified nod and proceeded to use them with considerably more restraint than her brother.

What Stormy's excavations taught me about Bengal bathroom engineering:

- Easy cleaning: Smooth surfaces without ridges where waste can hide
- Stability: Lightweight boxes become hockey pucks during vigorous use
- Open vs covered: Consider your Bengal's preference for visibility and airflow
- Multiple box strategy: Different locations prevent resource competition in multi-cat homes

What We Use and Why: After testing various options, we settled on large, high-sided open boxes made from smooth, durable plastic. Covered boxes created too much humidity and limited escape routes during multi-cat negotiations. Plus, Edan likes to supervise the cleaning process, which is impossible when I can't see her judgmental expressions.

Remember: what works for us might not suit your Bengal's preferences. Be prepared to experiment and keep receipts. Always keep receipts when shopping for Bengals.

"Many Bengal owners have found success with a range of litter box styles and brands. Here are some popular options to help you start your search; remember, what works for one cat might not work for another."

Bengal Owners Litter Box Styles		
Brand / Model	Features	Notes
Litter-Robot	Self-cleaning, large, open design	Great for multi-cat homes
Catit Jumbo Hooded	Spacious, covered, carbon filter	Good for privacy-loving Bengals
Modkat XL	High sides, top or front entry	Stylish, easy to clean
PetSafe ScoopFree	Self-cleaning, disposable trays	Low maintenance, less odor

Carriers: The Great Transport Negotiation

The first time I attempted to transport Edan and Stormy to the vet in separate carriers, I learned that Bengal diplomatic relations are more complex than I'd anticipated. Edan entered her carrier with resigned dignity but immediately began a vocal protest that sounded like a diplomatic complaint being filed with the United Nations. Stormy, witnessing his sister's distress from his adjacent carrier, launched into supportive commentary that turned our car into a mobile concert hall.

Halfway to the vet, inspiration struck. At the next traffic light, I carefully transferred Stormy into Edan's larger carrier. The change was immediate and remarkable; the protests stopped, replaced by mutual comfort behaviors. They settled against each other, offering moral support through synchronized purring and strategic positioning for maximum security.

Now our annual vet visits feature the shared carrier system. They travel like a small support group, facing veterinary adventures together rather than enduring the stress of separation during already stressful situations. The larger carrier comfortably fits both cats while providing them with the emotional security of companionship.

What the Transport Negotiation taught me about Bengal carriers:

- **Standard carrier:** Suitable for average cats who accept cramped conditions
- **Bengal carrier:** Must accommodate a cat who believes personal space is a fundamental right
- **Multi-Bengal carrier:** For cats who provide each other moral support during stressful journeys

The Shared Carrier Discovery: Our yearly vet visits taught me that Edan and Stormy travel better together than apart. Watching them provide mutual moral support during car trips is like witnessing a tiny furry support group. *"We're in this together"* seems to be their motto, usually delivered through synchronized purring and strategic positioning for maximum comfort.

Additional Bengal Transport considerations:

- **Hard vs soft carriers:** Hard for escape artists, soft for cooperative travelers
- **Emergency backup:** When Bengal engineering defeats your primary option
- **Security testing:** Test latches before travel day, "escape-proof" is a challenge, not a guarantee
- **Familiar comfort items:** Blankets and treats ease travel stress

Pro tip: Test carrier security before travel day. Bengals view "escape-proof" as a personal challenge rather than a product guarantee.

Cat Carrier Types & When to Use		
Carrier Type	**Best For**	**Legal Notes / Travel Tips**
Soft Carrier	Car trips, vet visits	Legal for cars/public transport, not cargo air
Hard Carrier	Air travel, long trips	Required for cargo air, safest for strong cats

Chapter 15
Resources and Shopping Guide

Food and Water Bowls: The Bengal Culinary Experience

The Great Bowl Migration Incident

When I first brought home what I thought were practical food bowls, lightweight ceramic dishes from a pet store that promised *"easy handling and attractive design."* I was feeling quite prepared for Bengal dining needs. That confidence lasted exactly one breakfast.

Stormy approached his morning meal with his usual methodical enthusiasm. He sniffed, approved, and began eating with the focus of a food critic conducting a serious review. Halfway through his breakfast, as he repositioned himself for optimal kibble access, his bowl suddenly shot across the kitchen floor like a ceramic hockey puck, trailing kibble and leaving Stormy staring at the spot where his breakfast used to be.

I watched in amazement as he followed the bowl's trajectory, then sat down beside it and gave me a look that clearly said, *"Your dining room management needs serious improvement."* This wasn't cat clumsiness; this was a design flaw in my bowl selection strategy.

That afternoon, I invested in heavy stainless-steel bowls that could withstand Bengal dining enthusiasm. Stormy tested them immediately, conducting his usual pre-meal positioning routine. The bowls stayed put. He ate with dignity restored, and I learned that successful Bengal feeding requires equipment that can handle their athletic approach to dining.

What the Bowl Migration taught me about Bengal dining equipment:

- **Wide and shallow design:** Reduces whisker fatigue and allows comfortable eating positions
- **Easy cleaning:** Dishwasher-safe materials that don't retain odors or stains
- **Non-slip bases:** Work with weight to prevent sliding during athletic eating sessions
- **Individual preferences:** Test different materials, some cats prefer ceramic, others steel

Bengal Food Critic Reviews: Edan approaches new food with the discernment of a Michelin-starred restaurant critic. She'll sniff, sample a single kibble, and either purr approval or deliver a withering look that clearly communicates *"This is beneath my standards."* Stormy's review process involves eating everything enthusiastically, then deciding afterwards whether it met his expectations.

The Expensive Food Paradox: I've learned that the price of cat food is inversely proportional to Bengal enthusiasm. The $80 premium salmon pâté gets a polite nibble, while the free sample of budget kibble becomes an instant obsession. It's like they have a built-in expensive-taste detector that operates in reverse.

Chapter 15
Resources and Shopping Guide

Stormy's Bowl Review: *"After extensive testing, I can confirm that lightweight bowls are excellent for entertainment but terrible for dignified dining. Heavy bowls stay where you put them, which is essential for proper meal presentation. Also, automatic feeders are suspicious and require thorough investigation before trust can be established."*

"To make shopping easier, here are some bowl brands and types that other Bengal owners use. Feel free to compare features and find what fits your Bengal's needs and your home."

Food & Water Bowls		
Brand / Model	**Features**	**Notes**
Catit	Stainless steel, whisker-friendly	Easy to clean, affordable
Pioneer Pet	Ceramic, wide shallow bowls	Prevents whisker fatigue
PetFusion	Non-slip, modern design	Heavy, hard to tip over
PetSafe Drinkwell	Water fountain, filtered	Encourages hydration

303

Food Types: Navigating Bengal Nutritional Preferences

Dry, Wet, and Raw: The Great Food Debate

There's no single 'best' food for every Bengal, but these brands are commonly chosen by Bengal owners. Use this as a starting point and consult your vet for tailored advice.

Popular Food Brands for		
Brand	**Type**	**Notes**
Royal Canin Bengal	Dry	Breed-specific, balanced nutrition
Applaws	Wet/Dry	High meat, grain-free
Ziwi Peak	Air-dried/raw	High-protein, limited ingredients
Black Hawk	Dry	Australian, natural ingredients
Feline Natural	Freeze-dried	Raw, high-protein, easy to store

Dry Food Options:

- Convenient for puzzle feeders and training treats
- Look for high-protein, grain-free formulations
- Essential for dental health when used alongside wet food
- Perfect for Bengal food critics who like to sample individual kibbles.

Chapter 15
Resources and Shopping Guide

Wet Food Benefits:

- Provides essential hydration for kidney health
- Usually, it is more appealing to picky Bengal palates
- Easier to disguise medications when needed
- Allows for more dramatic food presentation preferences.

Raw Feeding Considerations:

- Closest to a natural diet, but requires careful preparation
- Consult veterinarians and experienced raw feeders
- Significant time investment, but often excellent results
- Appeals to Bengals who appreciate authentic hunting experiences.

Portion Control: Feeding Athletes

Bengal Portion Reality: These aren't sedentary lap cats; they're feline athletes who burn calories through constant movement and mental activity. Portion guidelines need adjusting for Bengal energy levels, midnight zoomies, and curtain-climbing expeditions.

Factors Affecting Portions:

- Age and activity level (kitten zoomies vs. adult strategic planning)
- Indoor vs. supervised outdoor access
- Individual metabolism (Edan burns calories thinking, Stormy conserves energy efficiently)
- Seasonal activity changes (winter napping vs. summer adventures)

Adjust portions for activity, metabolism, and health. Always provide fresh water.

Bengal Age / Weight	Meals per Day	Amount per Day	Activity / Notes
Kitten 3–6mo (1–2kg)	3–4	60–120g (10% body wt)	Up portions for growth, split meals for energy
Kitten 6–12mo (2–3kg)	3	90–130g	Add more if growing fast or extremely active
Adult (3–5kg)	2–3	140–250g (3–5% bw)	+10–20% for high-zoomies, reduce for indoor-only
Senior (4–5kg, low act)	2	110–180g	Seniors generally need 10–15% less; monitor for loss

At-a-Glance Bengal Feeding Table

Remember: Edan can burn through her daily calories in a single epic play session, while Stormy's methodical approach results in steadier energy consumption throughout the day. Adjust portions based on your Bengal's individual athletic career.

CHAPTER 15
RESOURCES AND SHOPPING GUIDE

Where to Find Raw Food and Specialty Diets

For Raw Feeding Enthusiasts:

Butcher Shops: Many owners source raw meat from local butchers; ask about pet-safe options and bulk discounts. Most butchers are happy to discuss appropriate cuts and preparation methods. Some even enjoy the challenge of creating Bengal-specific meal plans.

Specialty Pet Food Stores: Some carry frozen raw, freeze-dried, or premium grain-free foods designed specifically for carnivorous pets. Staff often have experience with alternative feeding methods.

Online Raw Suppliers: Search for local or regional raw pet food companies in your area:

- **Australia:** Raw & Fresh, Big Dog Pet Foods
- **USA:** Darwin's Natural Pet Products, Stella & Chewy's
- **Regional suppliers:** Often provide fresher products and better customer service

Always research suppliers thoroughly and follow food safety protocols when handling raw meat for pets. Your Bengal's health depends on proper preparation and sourcing.

Cat Trees: The Penthouse Purchase

When the delivery truck arrived with our floor-to-ceiling cat tree, I wasn't prepared for the inspection process that followed. Edan approached the massive structure like a real estate appraiser evaluating premium property. She tested each platform with delicate paw placement, examined the scratching posts for texture quality, and conducted what I can only describe as a structural engineering assessment of the support beams.

Stormy took a more cautious approach, observing from a safe distance before making his move. Once Edan had given her preliminary approval, he ventured over for his own evaluation. Within an hour, they'd established their territorial claims: Edan claimed the penthouse suite (the highest platform), while Stormy preferred the mid-level lounges with better kitchen supervision views.

Two years later, their *"Cat Empire"* dominates our living room. Edan still treats the top level like her royal throne room, while Stormy has perfected the art of dramatic entrances from the middle platforms. The investment paid off, not just in entertainment value, but in preventing them from turning my bookcases into climbing equipment.

Chapter 15
Resources and Shopping Guide

What the Penthouse Purchase taught me about Bengal furniture:

- **Multiple levels:** Different heights accommodate various moods and territorial preferences
- **Scratching surfaces:** Integrated scratching areas reduce furniture targeting
- **Replacement parts availability:** Worn scratching posts should be replaceable
- **Window placement:** Near windows provides entertainment value and bird-watching opportunities.

Size and Placement Considerations:

- Floor-to-ceiling models maximize vertical space but require earthquake-level stability
- Multiple smaller trees create territory options and reduce competition for the penthouse suite
- Placement near windows provides entertainment value and bird-watching opportunities
- Stability matters more than elaborate features; fancy doesn't survive Bengal testing

We've learned that expensive doesn't always mean better. Sturdiness and appropriate sizing trump fancy features every time.

"If you're wondering where to look for sturdy cat trees or climbing shelves, here are a few brands that Bengal owners often mention. These are just starting points; explore and see what suits your space and your cat's style."

Cat Trees & Vertical Play

Brand/Model	Features	Notes
Mau Lifestyle	Modern, sturdy, real wood	Blends with home décor
Vesper	Modular, replaceable parts	Soft memory foam cushions
Tuft + Paw	Designer cat furniture	Premium, high-end look
Catkea	Budget-friendly, easy to assemble	Good starter option

Scratching Solutions: The Furniture Defense Strategy

The first time I heard the distinctive sound of claws meeting expensive fabric, I knew my furniture education was about to become very expensive. Edan had discovered that my new sofa provided excellent scratching resistance, exactly the kind of challenging workout her claws apparently needed. Stormy, observing from his diplomatic distance, seemed to be taking notes for his own furniture evaluation session.

Within a week, one corner of the sofa looked like it had survived a small tornado. I realized I was fighting a battle I couldn't win without providing better alternatives. The next day, I strategically placed a tall scratching post right next to Edan's chosen scratching spot. She investigated, tested the

Chapter 15
Resources and Shopping Guide

texture, and gradually shifted her attention to the more satisfying sisal surface.

The key insight: Bengals don't scratch furniture to be destructive; they scratch because they need to scratch. Providing irresistible alternatives in the right locations redirects their natural behavior without suppressing it. Now we have multiple scratching posts throughout the house, and my furniture has survived two years of Bengal cohabitation.

What the Furniture Defense Strategy taught me about scratching solutions:

- **Multiple textures:** Sisal, carpet, and cardboard appeal to different preferences
- **Strategic placement:** Near sleeping areas, room entrances, and favorite hangouts
- **Height variety:** Tall posts for full body stretches, horizontal options for different angles
- **Replacement planning:** Worn scratching surfaces should be replaceable, not disposable

Grooming Tools: The Spa Equipment Selection

My first attempt at grooming Edan involved a generic pet brush from the grocery store and optimistic assumptions about Bengal cooperation. The session lasted approximately thirty seconds before Edan delivered a withering assessment of both my technique and my equipment quality. The brush pulled at her coat; the bristles were too harsh, and my amateur approach clearly didn't meet royal grooming standards.

A visit to the pet store educated me about the difference between *"pet brush"* and *"Bengal-appropriate grooming tools."* The rubber grooming mitt felt like a massage rather than maintenance, the fine-toothed metal comb caught tangles without pulling, and the soft bristle brush provided the finishing touches that earned Edan's purring approval.

Stormy's grooming preferences proved completely different; he preferred shorter sessions with a different brush texture and considerably more treat-based negotiations. This taught me that grooming tools, like everything else Bengal-related, require individual assessment and adaptation.

Chapter 15
Resources and Shopping Guide

What the Spa Equipment Selection taught me about grooming tools:

- **Rubber grooming mitts:** Feel like a massage, effective for loose hair removal
- **Fine-toothed metal combs:** Perfect for detail work and catching missed spots
- **Soft bristle brushes:** Gentle finishing touches that most cats enjoy
- **Individual preferences:** Different cats prefer different tools and techniques.

Safety Equipment: The Bengal-Proofing Hardware Store

The day I discovered Edan had learned to open the cabinet containing her treats marked the beginning of my education in Bengal-proof security systems. Standard child safety latches lasted exactly one determined investigation before being defeated by superior Bengal engineering skills. I found myself researching industrial-strength cabinet locks like I was securing state secrets rather than protecting cat treats.

The hardware store clerk initially seemed amused by my request for "cat-proof" security solutions, until I explained that these weren't ordinary cats. After hearing about Stormy's door handle operation skills and Edan's cabinet breakthrough techniques, he recommended magnetic locks, typically used for actual child safety, rather than the flimsy plastic versions I'd been trying.

Two years later, our house features a sophisticated security system designed around two small, intelligent creatures who view *"cat-proof"* as a personal challenge. Some days I feel like I'm living in a benevolent maximum-security facility, but at least the treats stay secure, and the dangerous items remain safely locked away.

What Bengal-Proofing Hardware taught me about safety equipment:

- **Magnetic cabinet locks:** Stronger than standard child safety latches
- **Outlet covers:** Essential for curious cats who investigate everything
- **Cord protectors:** Prevent chewing on dangerous electrical items
- **Secure storage:** For medications, small objects, and toxic substances

Chapter 15
Resources and Shopping Guide

Toys and Enrichment: The Entertainment Budget

Toys: The Cardboard Box Economics

The day I spent $80 on a sophisticated electronic mouse toy, I was convinced I'd solved Bengal entertainment forever. The toy featured multiple speeds, random movement patterns, and, according to the manufacturer, *"irresistible prey simulation."* Edan and Stormy approached it with polite interest, conducted a brief investigation, and rendered their verdict: mildly amusing for approximately fifteen minutes.

The cardboard box the toy arrived in, however, became the centerpiece of a six-month entertainment empire. Edan transformed it into her fortress headquarters, complete with strategic viewing ports she created through dedicated paw work. Stormy used it as his stealth operations base, perfecting his surprise attack techniques from within its depths.

This taught me the fundamental principle of Bengal toy economics: entertainment value operates on an inverse relationship to purchase price. The most expensive toys often become expensive dust collectors, while simple cardboard boxes, paper bags, and toilet paper tubes provide endless fascination for Bengal minds.

What Cardboard Box Economics taught me about Bengal toys:

- **Interactive wand toys:** Essential for daily play sessions and bonding
- **Puzzle feeders:** Mental stimulation that doubles as mealtime enrichment
- **Rotating toy collection:** Prevents boredom through novelty
- **DIY enrichment supplies:** Cardboard boxes, paper bags, toilet paper tubes

What Usually Failed:

- **Electronic toys without variability:** Interesting for a week, then ignored
- **Overly complex puzzle toys:** Frustration rather than entertainment
- Anything small enough to swallow: Safety hazard for curious cats
- **Toys that break easily:** Bengal enthusiasm tests all construction limits

Edan's Toy Philosophy: *"The best toys are the ones humans don't expect us to love. Expensive electronic mice are fine, but have you seen what I can do with a paper bag? Entertainment value is inversely related to purchase price. Also, if it costs more than $50, I'm legally obligated to ignore it for at least two weeks."*

Chapter 15
Resources and Shopping Guide

Stormy, the discerning Bengal, caught in his ultimate *"bug shopping"* ritual, testing durability, flavor, and, let's be honest, antenna-chew factor. Some products require more thorough investigation than others.

Shopping Strategy: The Receipt Reality

My first major Bengal shopping mistake involved a $150 puzzle feeder that promised to *"challenge even the most intelligent cats."* I spent hours researching, reading reviews, and convincing myself this was the perfect enrichment solution. When it arrived, Edan conducted her standard quality control inspection, which involved a thorough sniff test, structural assessment, and final verdict delivery.

Her review was delivered through strategic body language that clearly communicated: *"This color scheme is insufficient for royal dining experiences."* She walked away with the kind of dignified dismissal usually reserved for substandard service staff. Stormy, ever diplomatic, gave it a polite trial run before also declining to engage with the rejected equipment.

Fortunately, I'd kept the receipt and learned my first cardinal rule of Bengal shopping: always maintain return options when dealing with feline critics who operate on quality standards no human focus group could possibly anticipate. The rejected puzzle feeder returned to the store, and the refund funded several smaller experiments that actually met Bengal approval standards.

Research before you buy

What the Receipt Reality taught me about Bengal's shopping strategy:

Will this item survive Bengal athletic activities? (Translation: Can it withstand a 5kg missile launching itself from a 6-foot height at 3 AM?)

- Is it the right size for a larger, more active cat breed?
- Can it be easily cleaned or maintained after Bengal's *"quality testing"*?
- Are replacement parts available when (not if) components wear out?
- Does it serve multiple functions or solve multiple problems?

The Return Policy Reality: Always keep receipts when shopping for Bengals. Not because the products are defective, but because your feline quality control team operates on standards that no manufacturer could possibly anticipate. I once returned a perfectly good puzzle feeder because Edan deemed the color *"insufficient for royal dining experiences."*

Chapter 15
Resources and Shopping Guide

Where to Shop: The Great Shopping Discovery Journey

The Online Research Rabbit Hole: My first major Bengal shopping expedition started with what I thought would be a quick online search for *"best cat tree for large cats."* Three hours later, I had seventeen browser tabs open, a spreadsheet comparing features across twelve different brands, and the growing realization that I'd fallen down a research rabbit hole that had no bottom.

The problem wasn't a lack of information; it was too much information. Every product had glowing five-star reviews right next to scathing one-star warnings. One reviewer claimed their Bengal loved the exact same cat tree that another reviewer said their cat completely ignored. I was more confused after three hours of research than when I started.

Finally, I decided to combine approaches: research extensively online to understand features and prices, then visit our local pet store to see the actual products before making decisions. This hybrid strategy saved me from several expensive mistakes and helped me build a relationship with staff who actually understood active cat breeds.

Online Shopping Benefits:

- Broader selection and price comparison capabilities
- Reviews from other Bengal owners (filter for breed-specific feedback)
- Convenient delivery for bulky items like cat trees
- Often, better return policies for items that don't meet expectations

In-Store Shopping Advantages:

- Physical assessment of build quality and materials
- Immediate availability without shipping delays
- Supporting local businesses and getting personalized advice
- Ability to see actual size and proportions before Bengal inspection.

The Local Pet Store Heroes: The staff at our local Petbarn became my Bengal shopping consultants after I explained Edan and Stormy's unique requirements. When I mentioned that standard carriers were too small and regular litter boxes were inadequate for archaeological excavations, they immediately understood I wasn't dealing with typical house cats.

They started setting aside larger carriers when they came in and calling me when they received new high-sided litter boxes. This personal service made all the difference; instead of guessing from online photos, I had knowledgeable allies

Chapter 15
Resources and Shopping Guide

who understood Bengal-specific needs and could recommend products that actually worked for active, intelligent cats.

The International Shipping Reality Check: When I fell in love with a specific cat tree design only available from a UK retailer, I learned the hard way about international shipping costs for large items. The £200 cat tree became a $450 Australian investment after shipping, duties, and currency conversion. Edan's royal approval didn't quite justify the premium.

This expensive lesson taught me to focus on features rather than specific brands and to find local equivalents before considering international purchases. That same cat tree style was available from an Australian supplier for half the total cost; I just needed to search for features rather than brand names.

Our approach: research extensively online, then buy locally, when possible, especially for large items that benefit from seeing in person. This also supports local businesses that understand the unique challenges of Bengal ownership.

Online Retailers: Global, America, and Australia

Global Shopping Strategy:

- Focus on features and specifications rather than specific brand names
- Factor shipping costs and duties into price comparisons

- Search for local equivalents before ordering internationally
- Join regional Bengal owner groups for location-specific recommendations

Global Options:

- Amazon: International availability varies by product, with an extensive selection
- Specialty pet retailers: Often offer worldwide shipping for unique items
- Manufacturer direct sales: Best for specialty items like cat wheels or custom furniture

United States:

- Chewy: Extensive selection, fast shipping, excellent customer service
- Petco/PetSmart: National chains with online presence and local pickup options
- Regional specialty retailers: Often carry unique items not found elsewhere

The Australian Bengal Shopping Network: Through online Bengal communities, I discovered that other Australian owners had already done the legwork of finding quality suppliers. They recommended Pet Circle for online ordering with fast delivery, Petbarn for hands-on product assessment, and My Pet Warehouse for bulk litter purchases that make sense with two cats.

Chapter 15
Resources and Shopping Guide

The most valuable discovery was that local pet stores often special-order items not in regular stock. When I couldn't find the specific puzzle feeders other Bengal owners recommended, our local store ordered them in, sometimes at better prices than online retailers.

Where Australian Bengal owners shop successfully:

- Petbarn/Greencross: National coverage with both online and physical stores
- Pet Circle: Online specialist with competitive pricing and fast delivery
- My Pet Warehouse: Bulk options available, good for multi-cat households

Community Shopping Wisdom: The best shopping advice came from other Bengal owners in similar situations. Urban apartment dwellers recommended different suppliers than rural property owners, and multi-cat households had different bulk buying strategies than single-cat families. This community knowledge saved me from numerous shipping mistakes and led me to suppliers I never would have found through general internet searches.

Our approach now: research extensively online, then buy locally, when possible, especially for large items that benefit from hands-on assessment. This supports local businesses that understand the unique challenges of Bengal ownership while ensuring we get products that actually work for our specific cats.

Online Retailers: Global, America, and Australia

Store Name	Region	What They Offer	Notes
Chewy	USA	Huge selection of food, litter, toys, health	Fast shipping, auto-ship discounts
Amazon	Global	Wide range of brands, reviews, fast delivery	Check seller ratings, easy returns
Petco	USA	Food, litter, toys, furniture, live chat support	In-store pickup available
PetSmart	USA	Food, litter, toys, grooming, live pets	Loyalty rewards, curbside pickup
Pet Circle	Australia	Food, litter, toys, health, auto-delivery	Australian brands, fast shipping
PETstock	Australia/NZ	Food, litter, toys, grooming, vet services	In-store and online, loyalty club
My Pet Warehouse	Australia	Food, litter, toys, beds, carriers	Frequent sales, click & collect
Zooplus	Europe/UK	Premium food, litter, toys, specialty brands	Ships to many countries
Petbarn	Australia	Food, litter, toys, grooming, adoption	In-store clinics, online ordering
BudgetPetProducts	Australia	Food, flea/tick, health, toys	Discount prices, fast delivery
Pet Circle	Australia	Auto-delivery, wide range, local support	Good for recurring essentials
Fitfuncatwheel	Australia/NZ	Cat wheels	Distributor of the Ferris Cat Wheel

Tip: For international shipping, check each store's policy; some will ship selected products globally, while others are region-specific. Factor in shipping costs when comparing prices.

Chapter 15
Resources and Shopping Guide

For indoor Bengal adventures, I highly recommend the Fit 'n' Fun Cat Wheel—Edan's favourite daily exercise and an absolute lifesaver when the midnight zoomies hit. The company's customer service is top notch, making the whole experience as smooth as Edan on her third lap. You can check it out and buy yours at the official website: https://fitnfuncatwheel.com/bengalguide

(where endless Bengal energy meets its match).

International Shopping Considerations

Regional Availability Variations

Product availability varies significantly between countries. Brands popular in Australia might not be available in North America, and vice versa. Focus on features and specifications rather than specific brand names when researching options. Your Bengal cares about function, not brand prestige.

Finding Local Alternatives:

- Use features and specifications to find local equivalents
- Contact local pet stores about special ordering capabilities
- Join regional Bengal owner groups for location-specific recommendations
- Check with veterinarians for trusted local supplier recommendations

Popular Bengal Enrichment Products: Australian Starting Points

New Bengal owners often ask what specific products work well for active, intelligent cats. These brands are commonly available in Australia and have received positive feedback from Bengal families, but remember: your Bengal will be the ultimate judge of what becomes a favorite!

Interactive Electronic Toys:

- **MayMaw KiTiFISH:** Motorized fish toy for solo hunting practice
- **SmartyKat Hot Pursuit:** Electronic wand toy with unpredictable movement
- **PetSafe Bolt Laser:** Automatic laser for independent play sessions
- **Catit Senses Play Circuit:** Modular track system for chasing games

Natural Chew and Comfort Options:

- **Silvervine sticks:** Natural alternative to catnip (various Australian suppliers)
- **KONG Cat Dental Chews:** Durable chewing satisfaction
- **Petstages Dental Health Chews:** Texture variety for different preferences

Chapter 15
Resources and Shopping Guide

Shopping Strategy: Product availability varies across Australian states and online retailers. Focus on the features that matter: interactive movement, appropriate sizing for larger cats, and durable construction, rather than specific brand names. Many pet stores can special-order items not in stock.

Remember: The most expensive toy often loses to a cardboard box, so start with one or two items to learn your Bengal's preferences before investing in a full collection.

The Economics of Bengal Ownership

Budget Planning Reality Check

Categories Where Quality Matters:

- **Health care:** Never compromise on veterinary care or emergency funds
- **Food:** High-quality nutrition is a long-term investment in health
- **Safety equipment:** Carriers, harnesses, and climbing furniture should prioritize durability
- **Litter boxes:** Buy once, use for years, invest in an appropriate size and quality

Where You Can Save Money:

- Toys: DIY options often work as well as expensive alternatives
- Bedding: Bengals prefer your clothes anyway; expensive beds aren't necessary
- Feeding accessories: Basic heavy bowls work better than fancy automatic feeders

CHAPTER 15
RESOURCES AND SHOPPING GUIDE

The Hidden Costs Reality

Expenses You Might Not Anticipate:

- **Replacement costs:** Bengal enthusiasm means items wear out faster
- **Emergency veterinary care:** Active, curious cats face more accident risks
- **Home modifications:** Cat-proofing and enrichment additions add up
- **Travel arrangements:** Pet-friendly accommodations and sitters cost more

Budget for 20-30% above your initial estimates. Bengal ownership includes surprise expenses that aren't always predictable, like replacing blinds after they become climbing equipment or investing in industrial-strength cabinet locks.

Tips for Comparing Products

The Bengal-Specific Evaluation Process

1. **Prioritize Your Bengal's Needs:** Consider your cat's age, size, and preferences (does your Bengal love to climb or prefer cozy hideouts?). Think about your home's layout and where you'll place items.
2. Check Product Features:
    - Size & Capacity: Make sure items are big enough for an athletic Bengal

- Materials: Look for sturdy, non-toxic materials that survive Bengal testing
- Ease of Cleaning: Removable covers and wipeable surfaces save sanity
- Safety: Avoid products with small detachable parts or sharp edges

3. **Read Reviews from Bengal Owners:** Search for feedback from other Bengal owners; what works for a Persian might not survive Bengal athletics.
4. **Compare Price and Value:** Don't just go for the cheapest option; consider longevity and replacement costs. Sometimes paying more for quality saves money and frustration long-term.
5. **Test Return Policies:** Choose retailers with generous return policies for items that don't meet Bengal approval standards.

Chapter 15
Resources and Shopping Guide

Community Connections: The Bengal Owner Support Network

Finding Your Tribe

Bengal owner groups operate like support groups for people whose cats have opinions about everything. *"My cat has redesigned my living room again"* and *"Help, my Bengal has learned to open doors"* are considered normal conversation starters. These communities become essential when you need someone who understands why you're researching industrial-strength cabinet locks at 2 AM.

Where to Connect:

- Online forums and Facebook groups: 24/7 advice and camaraderie
- Breed-specific meetups and cat shows: Face-to-face connections
- **Local Bengal breeders:** Often maintain owner networks and support groups
- **Veterinary clinics:** That specialize in active breeds

No one understands a Bengal owner like another Bengal owner! Join online forums, attend breed meetups, and share stories. There's always someone who's faced your exact challenge and lived to laugh about it.

The Bengal Individual Difference Principle

Remember: Every Bengal is unique. What works for Edan or Stormy might not be your cat's favorite. Use these recommendations as starting points to compare, experiment, and find the best fit for your Bengal and your home.

This applies to everything from food preferences to toy choices to sleeping arrangements. Your Bengal will let you know their opinions, often in very creative ways that might involve strategic placement of rejected items in inconvenient locations.

Activity: Bengal Shopping Success Tracker

Before You Buy:

- What specific problem am I trying to solve?
- Have I researched alternatives and compared features?
- Does this item's size and construction suit Bengal's energy levels?
- What's my backup plan if this doesn't work?

After Purchase:

- Which items are getting regular use vs. being ignored?
- Are any items showing wear patterns suggesting replacement needs?
- What modifications would improve the current setup?

Chapter 15
Resources and Shopping Guide

- Which purchases would I definitely buy again vs. those I'd choose differently?

Monthly Review:

- Track which purchases provide ongoing value
- Note seasonal preference changes
- Document successful brand discoveries
- Plan future purchases based on proven preferences.

Stormy, the discerning Bengal, is caught in his ultimate "bug shopping" ritual, testing durability, flavor, and, let's be honest, antenna-chew factor

Edan's Perspective:

"Shopping for Bengals requires understanding that we have sophisticated preferences and athletic requirements. Cheap, flimsy items are insulting to our intelligence and physical capabilities. Invest in quality basics, then let us tell you what additional entertainment options meet our standards. Also, the box everything comes in is automatically mine, regardless of what's inside."

Stormy's Perspective:

"The best purchases are the ones that make daily life more comfortable and interesting without overwhelming us with unnecessary complexity. I prefer well-made items that last, comfortable resting spots that stay in good condition, and humans who understand that our approval can't be bought, it must be earned through thoughtful selection and adequate treat compensation."

Chapter 15
Resources and Shopping Guide

Final Thoughts

Shopping for Bengals is about understanding their unique needs and your specific household dynamics rather than following universal recommendations. What works brilliantly for one Bengal family might completely fail for another, depending on individual cat personalities, living situations, and household priorities.

The key insight from our shopping journey: invest in understanding what your specific Bengal values most, then prioritize quality in those areas while being creative and flexible about everything else.

Remember that the most expensive item isn't always the best choice, but the cheapest option rarely meets Bengal standards for durability and function. Focus on features that matter for active, intelligent cats, and don't be swayed by marketing claims that don't address real-world Bengal behaviors.

Your best shopping resources are other Bengal owners who share similar living situations and challenges. Connect with local Bengal communities, join online groups, and don't hesitate to ask specific questions about product performance and longevity.

Most importantly, maintain your sense of humor about the shopping process. Bengals have strong opinions about everything, and those opinions don't always align with human logic or manufacturer expectations. Part of Bengal ownership is learning to appreciate their unique perspectives on what constitutes quality, entertainment, and comfort.

Every day with a Bengal is a new adventure, sometimes wild and always wonderful. The right products can enhance that adventure, but the wrong expectations can lead to expensive disappointment. Shop smart, stay flexible, and remember cardboard boxes are always a safe bet.

The printable resources accompanying this chapter provide practical tools for organizing your shopping research, tracking product performance, and making informed decisions about future purchases. Use them to create your own Bengal-specific shopping wisdom that reflects your household's experiences and discoveries.

CHAPTER 15
RESOURCES AND SHOPPING GUIDE

 Bengal's Wild Ancestry and Bold Spirit

Born from the spirit of the Asian leopard cat, every Bengal carries the wild in their heart, reminding us to dream boldly, play fiercely, and see the tiger within ourselves, no matter our size

Conclusion

If you've made it this far, congratulations! Either you've survived Edan and Stormy's tales of chaos, or you're already deep in the wild world of Bengal ownership. Maybe both. This book was never meant to be a read-once-and-forget-it kind of manual. It's your trusty map, your late-night troubleshooting hotline (minus the hold music), and your cheerleader for every step of your Bengal's life, from that first *"should I?"* moment right through to senior snuggles.

We've covered a lot together, haven't we? You started by weighing if Bengals are your cup of tea (or triple espresso). Then you Bengal-proofed your home, hunted down ethical breeders or rescues, and learned the fine art of welcoming a new feline who thinks they own the place, because they do. We decoded those wonderfully bizarre Bengal behaviors: zoomies, water obsession, and opera-level yowling that could wake the dead.

You picked up tips on nutrition (including the art of feeding feline food critics), health checks, and litter box diplomacy. You mastered training basics and enrichment games that would challenge a rocket scientist and even tackled the delicate dance of introducing Bengals to kids, dogs, or other cats without requiring international mediation. Finally, we explored routines for lifelong happiness and how to stay plugged into the Bengal community, because you'll need witnesses to the daily entertainment.

CONCLUSION

What You're Walking Away With

You're leaving with so much more than random trivia about leopard-spotted cats. You've got your QR code resources for tracking and planning, the behavior troubleshooting table for those 3 AM mysteries, plant safety guides for your botanical detective work, and all the socialization strategies you'll ever need for managing a household diplomat with strong opinions about everything.

You know what to do when your Bengal chews on your headphones (apparently, they're testing audio quality), decides the kitchen sink is their new spa (water temperature inspection is serious business), or conducts 3 AM curtain-climbing demonstrations (athletic training never stops). You're ready for the curveballs, the *"uh-oh"* moments, and the victories, big and small.

This stunning image captures everything about Bengal ownership, athleticism, the confidence, the reach for something just beyond the ordinary. Every Bengal journey is unique, but they all lead to moments of pure joy and amazement like this.

"Every Bengal journey is unique, but they all lead to moments of pure joy like this."

The Truth About Bengal Life

Here's what I know after years with Edan and Stormy: Bengals will surprise you. Sometimes you'll be frustrated when you discover your cat has learned to open the treat cupboard and conducted a midnight quality control session. Sometimes you'll wonder if your cat is part monkey, part mastermind, part entertainment director. That's completely normal. Every Bengal owner has stories (and possibly a few missing socks, hair ties, and their dignity).

But with patience, preparation, and the right tools, you'll build a relationship that's full of laughter, affection, and daily adventures. You'll become an expert in cat-proofing, toy rotation, and the fine art of interpreting seventeen different types of meows and chirps. You'll also join a global family of Bengal owners who understand that *"my cat opened the cabinet again"* is a legitimate emergency text at any hour.

Keep Growing Together

Keep learning, because your Bengal will change and grow, and your routines should evolve too. Explore new games, update your enrichment plans, and don't be afraid to try something different. Celebrate those milestones: your first successful clicker trick, your first peaceful nap with the family dog, your first vet visit with zero drama, and that magical moment when your Bengal brings you their favorite toy as a gift.

Snap photos, keep a diary, and let yourself be proud of how far you've both come. Document the journey, you'll want to remember the chaos fondly when your wild kitten becomes a dignified senior cat who still occasionally demonstrates their vertical Olympic skills.

Welcome to the Family

No two days with a Bengal are ever the same. Some mornings, you'll wake up to purring cuddles and gentle headbutts. Other days, you'll discover that your Bengal has redesigned your living room overnight or decided that 5 AM is the perfect time for vocal warm-ups. Both experiences are part of the magnificent chaos that is Bengal ownership.

You're joining a community that spans the globe, Bengal lovers who are always ready to share advice, celebrate milestones, laugh at the latest feline antics, and provide emergency support when your cat discovers how to turn on the bathroom tap. We've

Conclusion

Edan's Final Perspective:

"If you've read this far, you're clearly serious about providing appropriate royal treatment. Remember: we choose our humans as much as you choose us. I expect daily entertainment, quality cuisine, and proper appreciation for my athletic demonstrations. Welcome to the Bengal family, prepare for a lifetime of supervision, amusement, and the occasional 3 AM quality inspection of your sleeping technique."

Stormy's Final Perspective:

"Every Bengal is different, but we all want the same things: comfort, adventure, and humans who understand that we're not just pets, we're family members with very specific standards and excellent ideas about home improvement. Enjoy the journey; we know we will. And remember, the best moments happen when you least expect them."

Your Adventure Begins Now

Thank you for letting Edan, Stormy, and me be part of your Bengal adventure. I started out just like you, curious, nervous, and completely unprepared for the reality of living with feline royalty who have architectural opinions and scheduling preferences. Now, with two spotted teachers providing daily lessons in humility, creativity, and unconditional love, I wouldn't trade this journey for anything.

You've got this. Trust your instincts, enjoy the ride, keep your sense of humor intact, and give your Bengal an extra chin scratch from all of us. Welcome to the wonderful, wild world of Bengal ownership, where every day is an adventure and your cat is both the star and the director of the show.

Here's to the beginning of your Bengal story. Make it a good one.

"Don't forget: *All the tools referenced in this guide are waiting in your free resource collection. Scan the QR code on page 2 to access your complete Bengal owner toolkit."*

Acknowledgements

Writing this guide has been both a joy and a challenge, and I am deeply grateful to those who supported me along the way.

To my beta readers — Robyn Nielsen, Lisa Lewis, Lynn Downd, and Kelly Blatz— thank you for your thoughtful feedback, encouragement, and keen eye for detail. Your insights helped shape this book into a practical and accessible resource for first-time Bengal owners.

I also wish to acknowledge the wider Bengal community, whose shared experiences and passion for the breed continually inspire me.

Finally, to Edan and Stormy, my spirited companions — this book would not exist without your endless curiosity, mischief, and love.

References & Further Reading

The following resources provide additional information on topics covered in this guide. Please note that websites, contact information, and availability may change over time. Always verify current information before relying on these resources.

Sources Referenced in This Guide

Expert Consultation:

- Lyn Dowd, Metanoia Bengals
  Richmond, Tasmania, Australia
  Breeding expertise, raw feeding safety protocols, and harness training recommendations

Recommended Products Mentioned:

- Butterfly Jacket Harnesses - Etsy (UK-made Velcro-fit harnesses)
- Tractive GPS Trackers - For supervised outdoor adventures
- Fit n Fun Cat Wheel – For the ultimate energy outlet for Bengals.
  https://fitnfuncatwheel.com/bengalguide
- MayMaw KiTiFISH - Motorized fish toy for interactive play
- SmartyKat Hot Pursuit - Electronic wand toy with unpredictable movement

References & Further Reading

- PetSafe Bolt Laser - Automatic laser for independent play sessions
- Catit Senses Play Circuit - Modular track system for chasing games

Digital Tools Mentioned:

- PictureThis - Plant identification with toxicity warnings
- ToxiPets - Pet-specific plant safety app
- Pet Protect Plan: Toxic Plant - Toxicity database
- LeafSnap - Botanical identification tool
- ASPCA Animal Poison Control Center App - Official poison control resource

Veterinary and Health Resources

Feline Health Organizations

- American Association of Feline Practitioners (AAFP) www.catvets.com - Comprehensive feline health information and veterinarian directory
- International Cat Care icatcare.org - Evidence-based cat health and behavior resources
- Australian Veterinary Association www.ava.com.au - Professional veterinary guidance and clinic directory

Bengal-Specific Health Information

- The International Cat Association (TICA) www.tica.org - Official breed standards and health testing information
- Feline Health Center, Cornell University www.vet.cornell.edu/animal-health-diagnostic-center/programs/feline-health-center
- UC Davis Veterinary Genetics Laboratory vgl.ucdavis.edu - Genetic testing for hereditary conditions

Emergency Resources

Poison Control Hotlines:

- **Australia:** Animal Poisons Helpline - 1300 869 738
- **United States:** ASPCA Animal Poison Control - (888) 426-4435
- **United Kingdom:** Animal PoisonLine - 01202 509000

Breed Organizations and Registries

International Bengal Recognition

- The International Bengal Cat Society (TIBCS) www.bengalcats.co - Breed standards and educational resources
- The International Cat Association (TICA) www.tica.org - Official breed standards and show information
- Cat Fanciers' Association (CFA) www.cfa.org - Breed recognition and breeding guidelines

Regional Bengal Clubs

- Bengal Cat Club of Australia
  Contact TICA Australia for current information
- Bengal Breed Council (USA)
  Part of the CFA breed councils system

Feline Nutrition Resources

- Feline Nutrition Foundation - Evidence-based feline dietary information feline-nutrition.org
- World Small Animal Veterinary Association (WSAVA) - Global nutrition guidelines wsava.org/committees/nutrition-committee

- Association of American Feed Control Officials (AAFCO) www.aafco.org - Pet food nutritional standards

Raw Feeding Resources

- Raw Fed and Nerdy Facebook Group - Evidence-based raw feeding discussion and guidance
- Dr Karen Becker - Holistic veterinary nutrition information healthypets.mercola.com
- American Veterinary Medical Association (AVMA) - Raw diet safety guidelines avma.org

Commercial Food Evaluation

- Pet Food Advisor - Independent pet food reviews and analysis
  www.petfoodadvisor.com
- Clean Label Project - Pet food quality testing and ratings cleanlabelproject.org
- Association of American Feed Control Officials (AAFCO)
  www.aafco.org - Pet food nutritional standards

Food Safety Resources

- FDA Center for Veterinary Medicine - Pet food safety guidelines fda.gov/animal-veterinary
- Pet Food Institute - Industry safety standards and guidelines petfoodinstitute.org

Raw Food Suppliers

- **Australia:** Raw & Fresh, Big Dog Pet Foods
- **United States:** Darwin's Natural Pet Products, Stella & Chewy's

Brand Information Note: Specific brand mentions throughout this guide (Royal Canin, Ziwi Peak, Applaws, Black Hawk, Feline Natural) are included as examples only and do not constitute endorsements. Always consult current product information and veterinary guidance for feeding decisions.

Behavior and Training Resources

Professional Organizations

- Certified Cat Behavior Consultant (CCBC) www.ccpdt.org - Directory of certified feline behavior professionals
- Animal Behavior Society www.animalbehaviorsociety.org - Academic and professional behavior resources

Training Resources

- Karen Pryor Clicker Training
  www.clickertraining.com - Foundational clicker training principles
- Cat Behavior Associates - Pam Johnson-Bennett
  www.catbehaviorassociates.com - Professional cat behavior guidance

Plant Safety and Toxicity

Authoritative Plant Safety Resources

- ASPCA Toxic and Non-Toxic Plants Database
  www.aspca.org/pet-care/animal-poison-control/toxic-and-non-toxic-plants
- Pet Poison Helpline Plant Database
  www.petpoisonhelpline.com/poisons
- International Cat Care Plant Lists
  icatcare.org/advice/plants-poisonous-to-cats

Enrichment and Environmental Management

Research-Based Enrichment

- The Ohio State University Indoor Pet Initiative
indoorpet.osu.edu - Environmental enrichment for indoor cats
- Journal of Feline Medicine and Surgery
journals.sagepub.com/home/jfm - Peer-reviewed feline research

Practical Enrichment Resources

- Jackson Galaxy
www.jacksongalaxy.com - Practical enrichment and behavior solutions

Community Resources

Online Bengal Communities

- Bengal Cat World Facebook Group
Active international Bengal owner community
- Reddit r/bengalcats
www.reddit.com/r/bengalcats - Discussion forum for Bengal owners
- Bengal Cat Forum
www.bengalcatforum.com - Dedicated Bengal discussion platform

Local Resources

- Cat Shows and Meets
  Check TICA/CFA event calendars for regional gatherings
- Breeder Networks
  Contact regional TICA or CFA affiliates for breeder referrals

Shopping Resources

Australian Retailers

- Petbarn/Greencross - National pet store chain
- Pet Circle - Online specialist retailer
- My Pet Warehouse - Bulk purchasing options

International Retailers

- Chewy (USA) - Extensive selection with fast shipping
- Amazon - Global availability varies by product
- Specialty cat furniture makers - Mau Lifestyle, Tuft + Paw, Vesper

Recommended Reading

Feline Behavior Books

- *"Think Like a Cat"* by Pam Johnson-Bennett
- "Your Cat: The Owner's Manual" by Dr Marty Becker
- "Bengal Cats: A Complete Guide" by Dan Rice, DVM

References & Further Reading

Professional Development

- Fear Free Pets Certification - fearfreepets.com
- National Board of Certification for Animal Welfare www.nbcaw.org

Legal and Regulatory Information

Breeding and Ownership Regulations

- Local Council Regulations - Check with local government for breeding permits
- Import/Export Requirements - Government agriculture departments
- Pet Insurance Providers - Regional comparison sites for coverage options

Disclaimer

The resources listed here were current at the time of publication. The author and publisher are not responsible for changes to websites, contact information, or resource availability. Always consult with qualified professionals for veterinary, behavioral, or legal advice specific to your situation.

The inclusion of any resource in this list does not constitute an endorsement of their services or products. Readers should evaluate all resources independently and make informed decisions based on their specific circumstances.

How to Use These Resources

- **For Health Concerns:** Start with your local veterinarian, then consult breed-specific health organizations for additional information.
- **For Behavior Issues:** Begin with certified cat behavior professionals in your area, supplemented by reputable online resources.
- **For Community Support:** Join online Bengal communities for daily support and local breed clubs for in-person connections.
- **For Continuing Education:** Follow veterinary and behavioral journals for the latest research and evidence-based practices.
- **Important:** While online resources provide valuable information, they should never replace professional veterinary care or qualified behavioral consultation for serious issues.

Author Bio

Helen Renisch is a lifelong animal lover and Bengal cat devotee living in Australia with her two spirited Bengals, Edan and Stormy. Her journey began with Edan's wild curiosity and boundless energy, quickly transforming Helen from a casual cat owner into a passionate Bengal advocate. Inspired by the breed's intelligence and playfulness, she welcomed Stormy a year later, doubling the mischief and love in her home.

With a background in learning and development, Helen brings a teacher's heart and a storyteller's touch to her writing. Her book is filled with practical tips, checklists, and real-life anecdotes, drawn from daily adventures with Edan and Stormy, to make Bengal ownership accessible and fun for first-time cat parents.

Helen believes every Bengal deserves a home that understands their unique needs and celebrates their wild spirit. When not writing or inventing new enrichment games, she enjoys quiet cuddles with her cats and connecting with fellow Bengal enthusiasts.

Notes

www.ingramcontent.com/pod-product-compliance
Lightning Source LLC
Chambersburg PA
CBHW061205070526
44583CB00025B/3121